Clinical Research
in MENTAL
HEALTH

Clinical Research
in MENTAL HEALTH
A Practical Guide

Gordon J. G. Asmundson
Regina Health District, Saskatchewan

G. Ron Norton
University of Winnipeg

Murray B. Stein
University of California, San Diego

SAGE Publications
International Educational and Professional Publisher
Thousand Oaks ■ London ■ New Delhi

For information:

Sage Publications, Inc.
2455 Teller Road
Thousand Oaks, California 91320
E-mail: order@sagepub.com

Sage Publications Ltd.
6 Bonhill Street
London EC2A 4PU
United Kingdom

Sage Publications India Pvt. Ltd.
M–32 Market
Greater Kailash I
New Delhi 110 048 India

Printed in the United States of America

Library of Congress Cataloging-in-Publication Data

Asmundson, Gordon J. G.
  Clinical research in mental health : practical guide / by Gordon J. G.
Asmundson, G. Ron Norton, Murray B. Stein.
       p. cm.
Includes bibliographical references and index.
  ISBN 0-7619-2210-5
  1. Mental health—Research—Methodology. I. Norton, G. Ron, 1941- II.
Stein, Murray B., 1959- III. Title.
  RA790.8 .A84 2002
  616.89′007′2—dc21

                                    2002000217

This book is printed on acid-free paper.

02 03 04 05 10 9 8 7 6 5 4 3 2 1

Acquisitions Editor:	Jim Brace-Thompson
Editorial Assistant:	Karen Ehrmann
Production Editor:	Sanford Robinson
Copy Editor:	Kris Bergstad
Typesetter:	Siva Math Setters, Chennai, India
Indexer:	Molly Hall
Cover Designer:	Janet Foulger

To Aleiia and Kimberley—my daughter and wife—for filling
my life with beauty, and Ron and Murray—my mentors—for sharing
your infinite wisdom with me.
Gordon J. G. Asmundson

To Judy, my best editor, friend, and wife.
G. Ron Norton

To my research mentors—who showed me how to do it,
and to my research students—who remind me why I do it.
Murray B. Stein

Contents

Foreword

The present era is, perhaps, the golden age of clinical research. Societies around the world and particularly in North America have recognized the value of research to health- and mental health-related issues as contributing substantially to their well-being. Elected representatives in the United States have made clinical research the highest priority and have mandated a doubling of the budget of the National Institutes of Health over a 5-year period to be completed by 2003, and there is every reason to believe that healthy budgetary influences will continue. Thus, money exists at a federal level to support the clinical research effort in amounts never before dreamed of. And clinical scientists are not disappointing. Discoveries during the past decade have dramatically increased our knowledge of the nature and treatment of physical and mental disorders. In the area of mental disorders we have discovered new and effective treatments, both drug and psychological, for the large majority of mental disorders. From anxiety disorders to bipolar disorders we know that both pharmacological and psychological approaches have empirical support, and that they are often synergistic, as is the case with Bipolar Disorder. Furthermore, we are beginning to appreciate at a level unanticipated until recently that neurobiological and psychological aspects of mental disorders are inextricably interrelated. We have known for a long time that when we successfully treat mental disorders with drugs, we change not only brain function but also thoughts, feelings, and behaviors. But we have learned only recently that when we successfully modify thoughts, feelings, and behaviors with psychological treatments that we are also profoundly affecting brain function and possibly the structure of the brain. Learning more about the mechanisms of actions of successful treatment is informing us, as it must, about the nature of psychopathology.

We are also beginning to examine the workings of our health care delivery system. As the cost of providing health care, including behavioral health care, has spiraled, governments and policymakers have made it their job to examine more closely the ways in which behavioral health care services are provided. Although the primary goal until recently has been holding down costs, it is also very clear that these policymakers, representing the public, are ultimately interested in providing quality treatment at a reasonable price, and they want evidence that this is happening. These developments are providing a new context for the delivery of health and behavioral health services that highlight contributions of research on explicating the effectiveness and efficiency of our interventions. Individual practitioners are also being held accountable for their work in a way never before conceived. Indeed, all individuals involved in the health care effort recognize that the experiences of clinicians must be observed, verified, and accumulated through empirical practice and accountability. Theoretical and empirical developments must be tested in ways that will influence and be relevant to practitioners. Society has finally recognized that without the development of a cumulative body of knowledge on the effects of various interventions in the human services, we are doomed to a series of never-ending fads and promises.

For students and other individuals considering entering the exciting world of clinical research there is much to be gained. Young clinical scientists can make important new discoveries that will benefit individuals throughout the world, and gain considerable recognition for their efforts. Plus there is the excitement of discovery for its own sake. How does one enter this rewarding but demanding career? What are the mix of activities and experiences that produce a truly outstanding researcher? In this book by Gordon Asmundson, Ron Norton, and Murray Stein one can find many of those answers. This book goes beyond the technicalities of research methods and experimental design to answer such questions as, How do you develop appropriate questions? How do you find the right mentor (this is a particularly important question because many of the best-known clinical scientists may not turn out to be the best mentors)? How do you write a research proposal? And how do you communicate your findings to the public? Every young professional hoping to gain a foothold in the clinical research endeavor will benefit from the pages that follow.

David H. Barlow, Ph.D.
Center for Anxiety and Related Disorders
Department of Psychology
Boston University

Preface

Clinical research can be an extremely fascinating and rewarding pursuit. But, there is much to learn if one is to have a good understanding of why it is done, how it is done, and what it contributes to our understanding of human phenomena. Care must be taken in generating research ideas, drafting action plans, writing research proposals, learning about variables and research methods, using statistics, and communicating research findings to the larger scientific community.

If you are reading this book, you are probably thinking about, or in the process of, conducting research. Our hope is to present you with information and material that will not only further stimulate your interest but also enhance your self-confidence and ability to conduct, from start to finish, a sound piece of clinical research. It is our goal to explain the research process in sufficient detail to allow you, with practice and help from your mentor(s), to make important discoveries and contributions in your chosen field.

In the pages that follow, we share with you the information and insights passed on to us by our mentors (and, yes, our students). We speak candidly and draw from our own experiences to illustrate the connection between clinical research findings and everyday life. Throughout the text, we try to ask questions to provoke your curiosity about scientific inquiry as well as thoughtful reflection about the logic, methods, analysis, interpretation, and communication of your own research. Because our backgrounds are in the areas of psychology and psychiatry, these disciplines comprise the primary focus of our discussions; however, the principles and procedures that we touch on are applicable across a wide array of clinical disciplines.

We hope that this text not only proves to be a useful resource to you in your student or professional work but also that it serves to open your mind to the plentitude of research possibilities within the clinical realm. Likewise, we hope that you come away from this text feeling both encouraged and energized. It is with sincerity that we wish you success in "testing" your own research ideas.

Acknowledgments

We are indebted to Linda Picot for her invaluable assistance in preparing the manuscript for this book, and to two graduate students, Kristi D. Wright (M.A. candidate in Clinical Psychology) and Jennifer A. Boisvert, M.A. (Ph.D. candidate in Clinical Psychology) for keeping us on track with their insightful feedback.

PART I

Getting Started

1

An Introduction to Clinical Research

No one can conceive the variety of feelings which bore me onwards, like a hurricane, in the first enthusiasm of success. Life and death appeared to me ideal bounds, which I should first break through, and pour a torrent of light into our dark world. A new species would bless me as its creator and source; many happy and excellent natures would owe their being to me. No father could claim the gratitude of his child so completely as I should deserve theirs.

Mary Shelley (1818/1994)

Who conducts clinical research? Just (very) strange people who run around in lab coats with clipboards overflowing with questionnaires and electrodes spilling from every pocket? Not really. If you are reading this book, you are probably already involved in clinical research to some degree. You may, for example, be involved in several formal research projects either as part of your course work and training if you are a student, or in your practice if you are a clinician. As part of your clinical training and related activities you may be conducting research all the time, but just not calling it that. Indeed, every time you ask questions, such as, "Why is his back pain so persistent? What if I try to gradually expose him to the activities he is avoiding rather than just increasing his general physical activity levels?" or, "I have treated at least 20 people with tricotillomania. Why isn't she getting better? Is she more depressed than the others? Does depression affect treatment?" you are setting the stage for research.

Research really consists of only four essential components. These include

1. asking a question,

2. systematically collecting information to answer the question,

3. analyzing and interpreting the "data" you collect, and

4. communicating your findings to others, whether through informal meetings with colleagues, presentations at conferences, or publication in scientific journals.

The purpose of this book is to provide you with easy access to many of the practical issues that relate to the process leading from formation of a research idea (i.e., asking a question) through to presentation and publication of your findings. As well, we briefly touch on issues important to applying your research findings within the context of your clinical work. Though our primary focus is on research issues regarding conditions pertinent to clinical psychologists and psychiatrists, you will see that the principles we discuss are generally applicable across a variety of disciplines.

However, before turning our attention to these practical issues of clinical research, it is important to consider several other issues that will influence and guide your participation in the research enterprise. These include potential obstacles that can impede research desire and efforts, an overview of the history and purpose of the scientific approach, and the importance of a research mentor.

Potential Obstacles to Conducting Research

Many people who would like to conduct research are often intimidated by what they think they must do to get involved in a research project or program. Several years ago, one of us (G. R. N.) carried out an informal survey of psychologists and physicians working in clinical settings. The people surveyed were all attending a seminar he was giving on "How to Do Research." None of them had published anything (at least since graduate school). When asked why, the most common answer was, "I don't have time" (see Illustration 1.1). The next most common answer was that they didn't think they had the expertise. All of these people were professionals.

Illustration 1.1.   Potential Obstacles in Conducting Research

TIME
CONFIDENCE
MOTIVATION
SPACE
EQUIPMENT

They certainly did have the expertise. What they meant was either that they had not had experience or training in scientific methodology or that they had not used their training in years and were unsure of themselves.

Similarly, the busy schedules characteristic of undergraduate and graduate training also tax students' ability to find time to devote to research activities beyond that of their thesis work. And, for the student heavily involved in clinical training, research education is often not a primary focus of the curriculum, nor is there a guarantee that a mentor with strong interest, skills, and practical knowledge of clinical research will be readily accessible. Consequently, many students, perhaps the majority of those that we have been involved with over the years, are initially burdened by uncertainty about research. This, to a large degree, is one of the obstacles that we hope this book will help you to overcome.

Perceived lack of time and low confidence are very real obstacles to getting your hands dirty in the soil of research, but they are not insurmountable. Nor are the third and fourth most common obstacles—lack of motivation and lack of space and equipment. So, what can we do to overcome these? We have a few ideas that might work.

Time

Finding time to do research can be challenging. If you are like the people surveyed, you probably feel you don't have time to keep up with the literature in your field, let alone contribute to it. The good news is that doing research can, in many instances, actually require far less time than you might think. We sometimes joke that there is an unwritten code among researchers to exaggerate how demanding research is. Indeed, one of us reportedly has two graduate students hired to sleep for him so that he can spend countless wakeful hours in the lab (or writing at the local coffee shop), and another of us is rumored to be more than one person. These descriptors of our research personas, though in good humor, really do serve to perpetuate a myth that extraordinary means must be taken to get things done in the clinical research arena.

Likewise, we frequently hear researchers complain (often, but not always, in jest) that they were up through the wee hours of the morning writing grant proposals, analyzing data, writing papers, and the like. These kinds of statements also serve to make research seem mystical in some way and would scare anyone who is already overworked away from thinking about doing a research project. It sometimes seems that researchers, including ourselves, say these things to keep people from doing research! If people actually knew how manageable the time requirements for some research projects were, then many more would be doing it and we wouldn't be special (in our minds).

Confidence

The issue of time aside, whether you are a student or a practicing clinician, we hope to inspire confidence about your research abilities in several ways. Most important, we want to equip you with the basic skills necessary to help you to do the research you want to do. As well, we attempt to provide you with an understanding of many of the practical aspects related to research, from asking questions through disseminating your findings to others. Along the way, we provide numerous examples and illustrations of the importance of being involved in research. We also provide checklists, where possible, that will assist you in making certain that all essential steps in a given aspect of a research project are completed.

Motivation

The third most common obstacle to doing research is motivation. "Why do I need to do research? What will I or my patients gain from my finding time to spend on research? I can find the answers in professional journals, can't I?" These are questions that we have heard asked on numerous occasions, by both students and colleagues. The answers are neither simple nor straightforward. In Chapter 2 we spend more time on the primary question of "Why do research?" Here we provide a brief illustration that shows what can be gained from doing your own research.

We've heard many clinicians say that the articles they read in their professional journals are often irrelevant to the work they do in their offices, clinics, or hospitals. The most common complaint is that the patients studied bear little resemblance to the ones they see. To some extent this is true.

Many of the studies reported in psychological, psychiatric, and other health science journals are done on highly selected participants. For example, many of the studies we have done to address various aspects of Panic Disorder have excluded patients with major depression, chemical abuse, or other serious problems (e.g., Asmundson & Stein, 1994; Korn, Plutchik, & van Pragg, 1997; Overbeek, Rikken, Schruers, & Griez, 1998; Stein & Asmundson, 1994). This is done to study "pure," or uncomplicated, Panic Disorder. However, pure Panic Disorder is rarely seen by most clinicians. The research reported on "pure" samples is very important for defining the specific characteristics of disorders and the people who have them.

We also need to find out if what we know about pure samples is relevant to other groups. Clinicians are often in a prime situation to address questions that they have about the applicability of results from pure samples to the people they treat in the "real world" of clinical practice. This type of research may be done to contribute to the field at large. In many cases, however, it is initiated as a means of answering a practical question that the clinician has.

Space and Equipment

It is amazing how many of the great discoveries in the health field were made by individuals working alone with minimal workspace or equipment. Pasteur's germ theory is such an example (Pasteur, 1878). So is Darwin's theory of evolution (Darwin, 1859). Both of these scientists observed nature and asked simple questions. They then went about making systematic observations that either verified or negated their hypotheses. Their findings had profound and lasting effects on the way we view various aspects of humanity. There are hundreds of similar cases in the history of science.

It is also interesting that many of the great discoveries were accidental discoveries. Important discoveries don't have to be made exclusively in expensive, well-equipped laboratories. As you will see, the many different methods available to clinical researchers ensure that some questions can be answered with relatively little need of extra space or equipment. Most important are creative ideas and rigorous, systematic data collection, analysis, and interpretation.

Bottom Line

The bottom line is that we want to help you overcome these real and perceived obstacles—lack of time, confidence, motivation, and space and equipment—because we firmly believe that it is very important for people who work in clinical settings to conduct research and report their results. Why? Health care, regardless of specific focus, is a knowledge-based enterprise. So, as we learn more about specific pathologies and conditions, we change the way we assess and treat them. How do we learn? By asking questions, systematically collecting information, and analyzing and interpreting the information. That is, we learn through research that is conducted by ourselves or others. We also firmly believe that you have a number of great research ideas that, if carried out, will contribute significantly to the understanding and better treatment of those you are caring for or, in the case of students, are aspiring to care for.

Let's look at a real example from the field of education of how several people who were not trained in research initiated and conducted a very clever project that did not require a lot of time, space, or equipment. Why an example from education? The reason is simple! As you progress through this book it will become apparent that the important principles and procedures of research are applicable across disciplines. Understanding these general principles and procedures will give you a solid foundation from which to develop as a clinical researcher.

Recently, two third-grade teachers and their school's lower school computer teacher were discussing the importance of teaching children touch typing as part of their computer class. The teachers were aware that there had been some research on the topic that showed that children with good typing skills received higher marks on their papers when they were typed on a word processor. They also found that the research articles they read indicated that children who were taught keyboarding skills showed improvements in other areas, such as reading and writing. What the teachers did not know was how early they could successfully teach typing skills. The computer teacher had worked with children in the fourth grade and found them able to learn the necessary skills. But would it work for children as young as 7 and 8 years of age? That was their research question. They discussed their idea with other teachers and a couple of psychologists at local universities. Everyone felt the idea was worth researching.

Their next step was to design the project. Because they had little background in doing this kind of research, they approached one of the authors for advice. He helped them design a simple comparison study. They would randomly choose one of the two Grade 3 classes to be the *experimental group* (the group to receive the manipulation of interest) and the other to be the *control group* (the group that receives either no manipulation or one that is believed to have no effect). The experimental group received 20 to 30 minutes of daily training in keyboarding. The control group spent as much time in the computer room working on projects, playing games, and the like, but did not receive training in keyboarding. Before the actual training started, the children in both groups took a typing test to determine how fast and accurately they could type.

Not surprisingly, they could type only two or three words per minute (well below the speed they could achieve with handwriting). This was consistent with what the teachers had found in other research on typing training. The project lasted approximately one month. At the end of the month, all children were again tested. Their results showed that the children who had received training in keyboarding were significantly faster than the control subjects on the second test. In fact, the controls showed almost no improvement in their typing speed and accuracy.

As a result of these findings, two things happened. First, the children in the control group received training in keyboarding (and improved as much as the group originally receiving training!). Second, the teachers were asked to write a paper describing their study for their school's magazine. This article has been sent to teachers and principals in several other schools. This study is an excellent example of how easy and important research can be. The study did not require much additional time (except for several hours spent on planning and writing), and it led to practical changes to the way in which teaching programs were provided.

The Scientific Approach

All sound clinical research, regardless of its discipline of origin, is based on the scientific approach. Obviously, this approach is rooted in science. But what is science? Some authors (Solso & Johnson, 1994; Stanovich, 1998) have found this question easiest to answer by suggesting what it is not. Science is not defined by a particular subject matter, such as chemistry or physics. Nor is it defined by a particular set of apparatus, such as Bunsen burners, test tubes, or electron accelerators.

Rather, science can be defined as a systematic approach to observing phenomena in the universe with the fundamental purpose of providing publicly accessible answers to specific, solvable questions. We do this, across disciplines, in an effort to understand, explain, predict, and control the specific phenomena of interest. This relates back to our previous suggestion that research consists of asking a question, systematically collecting information to answer the question, analyzing and interpreting the data, and communicating the findings.

Illustration 1.2.   Fundamentals of the Scientific Approach

OBSERVE A PHENOMENON—COGNITIVE, BEHAVIORAL, OR PHYSICAL—IN THE UNIVERSE
MAKE OBSERVATIONS IN A SYSTEMATIC MANNER
COMMUNICATE RESULTS PUBLICLY

Implicit in our definition of science, and in our description of the fundamental and desirable components of research, are the following:

1. observing, or looking at, some phenomena in the universe,

2. doing so in a systematic way, and

3. communicating results in a public form where the methods and findings can be critiqued.

This, in a nutshell, is the scientific approach (see Illustration 1.2).

It sounds quite simple, doesn't it? In many respects, particularly those pertaining to the principles, it is. This does not mean, however, that the questions, the process, and the answers to those questions are easy to come by. Ingenuity, insight, and willingness to speculate must be accompanied by a firm understanding of scientific methods and principles and balanced with uncompromising honesty, rigorous attention to detail, careful interpretation of the data collected, and an ability to communicate effectively, without exaggeration, and efficiently. This is an ideal set of qualities that, if aspired toward, will contribute greatly to the quality and impact of your research.

Importance of a Mentor

The importance of having a mentor to guide you in your clinical research pursuits cannot be understated. In fact, we firmly believe that the mentor plays what might be considered the most critical role in one's development as an independent clinical researcher—that of guidance and encouragement. Obviously, you can learn clinical research methods, statistical techniques, and scientific reading, writing, and presentation skills via a number of written sources. But, it is the mentor who can, and has committed to, coach you on the many "do's and don'ts" of the research process, providing invaluable guidance. Also important, your mentor can stimulate and nurture your enthusiasm for the research process, particularly when things are not going on schedule or the way they should (an all-too-often occurrence when doing research).

Is our opinion regarding the importance of a mentor a unique one? It doesn't seem so. Indeed, other authors (e.g., Bausell, 1994) and the majority of our colleagues have expressed this opinion as well. In recent surveys of leaders in the fields of Anxiety Disorder (Norton et al., 2000) and pain (Asmundson, Hadjistavropoulos, & Antonishyn, 2001) research, as well as of recipients of young investigator awards (Norton, Norton, & Asmundson, 1999), the importance of the mentor is frequently mentioned.

To restate, a knowledgeable and dedicated mentor is of the utmost importance. But, what if you do not have a person who is both knowledgeable and skilled at clinical research *and* readily available to provide the guidance you need? This, unfortunately, is a common predicament, as not all mentors are created equally (Hoshmand, 1994; Lumsden, Grosslight, Loveland, & Williams, 1988). And, the good ones are often in high demand, are often busy with their own research activities, or are not even located in the same region as you. Our first recommendation, despite these potential setbacks, is that you seek out an established researcher who is known to be a good mentor. You might be reticent to do so. You might also be surprised to find that many established clinical researchers are quite happy to spend time answering your questions and encouraging your efforts. With the availability of new information technologies, such as e-mail, this need not necessarily be done in person.

But, you may ask, "How do I go about finding a person who will be able to help stimulate and nurture me in my research pursuits? What is the procedure?" Perhaps the best advice we can offer here is to suggest that you acquaint yourself, as thoroughly as possible, with the "potential mentor," carefully evaluating his or her research activities and interests, both past and current, as well as supervision experiences. How? Well, with regard to the person's research activities and interests, start by gathering information available through the person's department. Most academic and health care institutions have hardcopy and electronic (Web-based) information available about their faculty members' activities and interests. Follow this up with a literature search (see Chapter 3) pertinent to the person's publications. You might select a few of these and give them a read. With regard to supervision experiences, it is useful to speak directly with the person. Other invaluable sources of this sort of information are the person's current students and research associates. Talk to them and ask questions. Taking all of the information you have gathered from these sources into consideration will give you a pretty good overall picture of the potential mentor, his or her current pursuits, as well as mentoring style and abilities. Ideally, you want (a) interests compatible with your own, (b) high levels of research activity and productivity, and (c) an interpersonal and teaching style that is well matched with you.

If you decide to approach a potential mentor, be yourself. But, importantly, be prepared to ask specific questions and to outline what you are hoping to receive from the mentor. This will indicate that you have given forethought to your request and should improve your chances of getting the help you need and getting it on a sustained basis. The knowledgeable mentor is one who wants to guide, stimulate, and nurture your research experiences; so, present your case along these lines.

When sound mentorship is simply not available, access to practical information about various aspects of the research process is the next best thing. This applies to those who do not have a knowledgeable mentor. It also applies to those who do have a knowledgeable mentor in cases where that mentor is not available. We hope to provide what we believe to be some of the essentials in this book. And, we hope to provide it to you in a light, easy to digest, and encouraging way that will promote creative thinking, scientific rigor, and personal satisfaction. Clinical research is serious business, but this does not mean that it cannot be conducted in an easy-going environment. Mentoring you through a book is not an ideal solution. It does, however, serve to get you some of the answers you need, when you need them.

Overview of the Chapters

Throughout the book, we use examples of research projects, of forms such as those that might be necessary to obtain informed consent, and of how to access additional expertise. The reason for the examples is that we are trying to make this book as user-friendly as possible. The research examples we use will most often be drawn from our own work. This is not because we feel it is better than other work. Rather, it is work that we are most familiar with. We know how we came up with the ideas, why we designed the studies as we did, and the kinds of problems we experienced while doing the research. Much of this kind of information is not contained in written reports. We hope that, by using our own examples, we will make reading our book more pleasant and informative. Those of us who have taught research methodology know that there are built-in negative biases against learning research methodology—methodology is often thought of as being hard work and boring. It doesn't have to be, at least for the most part, and we hope our book proves that.

In this brief introduction, let us describe how our book is laid out and what you can expect to find. We have divided the book into three parts:

1. Getting Started

2. Data and Methods

3. Communicating Your Findings

In Part 1, Getting Started, we attempt to convince you that doing research can, in many cases, be easy, enjoyable, and very rewarding. We start by describing why you might want to do research (Chapter 2), followed by a discussion of how to generate good research ideas (Chapter 3), and how to evaluate the existing literature critically (Chapter 4). We end Part 1 by providing details on how to write a research proposal (Chapter 5) and how to address ethical issues (Chapter 6).

In the chapters in Part 2, Data and Methods, we get into more technical matters such as what constitutes data (Chapter 7), how data are collected (Chapter 8), different kinds of variables and some related research methods (Chapter 9), and foundations of data management and analysis (Chapter 10). Part 2 is not meant to provide a detailed and comprehensive coverage of these issues, such as you might find in advanced research design or methodology textbooks. Rather, we hope to provide a gentle introduction that can be supplemented by additional textbooks or related materials.

Finally, in Part 3, Communicating Your Findings, we describe how and why (Chapter 11) you should communicate your findings to others. We focus primarily on communications that do not require extensive experience or resources, but we also include communications at conferences and in journals (Chapter 12). This section provides guidance to those of you who do not have access to a mentor with experiences of this sort (and even to those who do) and should help guide you into a comfort zone that will allow you to communicate your findings, regardless of particular format, with confidence.

We hope this book helps you in your research endeavors and we look forward to reading about your findings and seeing your name in print!

References

Asmundson, G. J. G., Hadjistavropoulos, T., & Antonishyn, M. (2001). Profiles and perspectives of the leading contributors in the field of pain. *The Pain Clinic, 13,* 55–69.

Asmundson, G. J. G., & Stein, M. B. (1994). Vagal attenuation in panic disorder: An assessment of parasympathetic nervous system function and subjective reactivity to respiratory manipulations. *Psychosomatic Medicine, 56,* 187–193.

Bausell, R. B. (1994). Conducting meaningful experiments: 40 steps to becoming a scientist. Thousand Oaks, CA: Sage.

Darwin, C. R. (1859). On the origin of species by means of natural selection. London: John Murray.

Hoshmand, L. T. (1994). Supervision of predoctoral graduate research: A practice-oriented approach. *Counseling Psychologist, 22,* 147–161.

Korn, M. L., Plutchik, R., & van Pragg, H. M. (1997). Panic-associated suicidal and aggressive ideation and behavior. *Journal of Psychiatric Research, 31,* 481–487.

Lumsden, E. A., Grosslight, J. H., Loveland, E. H., & Williams, J. E. (1988). Preparation of graduate students as classroom teachers and supervisors in applied and research settings. *Teaching of Psychology, 15,* 5–9.

Norton, P. J., Asmundson, G. J. G., Cox, B. J., & Norton, G. R. (2000). Future directions in anxiety disorders: Profiles and perspectives of leading contributors. *Journal of Anxiety Disorders, 14,* 69–95.

Norton, P. J., Norton, G. R., & Asmundson, G. J. G. (1999). Under the microscope: Thoughts and perspectives of the recipients of CPA's First Annual President's New Researcher Awards. *Canadian Psychology, 40,* 39–46.

Overbeek, T., Rikken, J., Schruers, K., & Griez, E. (1998). Suicidal ideation in panic disorder patients. *Journal of Nervous and Mental Disease, 186,* 577–580.

Pasteur, L. (1878). Germ theory and its applications to medicine and surgery. *Comptes rendus de l'Academie des Sciences, lxxxvi,* 1037–1043.

Shelley, Mary. (1994). *Frankenstein.* Middlesex, England: Penguin. (Original work published 1818)

Solso, R. L., & Johnson, H. H. (1994). *An introduction to experimental design in psychology: A case approach* (4th ed.). New York: HarperCollins.

Stanovich, K. E. (1998). *How to think straight about psychology* (5th ed.). New York: Addison Wesley Longman.

Stein, M. B., & Asmundson, G. J. G. (1994). Autonomic function in panic disorder: Cardiorespiratory and plasma catecholamine responsivity to multiple challenges of the autonomic nervous system. *Biological Psychiatry, 36,* 548–558.

2

Why Do Research?

Why do people get involved in clinical research? What motivates them to take time from their busy schedules full of clinical training and clinical duties to devote to a research project or program? What do you think the reasons are? What are your reasons? We have asked this question of many people who spend a good portion of their day doing research. In response, we typically hear answers such as, "Because I had a mentor who encouraged me to ask basic questions about the treatments that I use and their effects on my patients," and, "I am curious by nature. Research is a fulfilling and rewarding way to satisfy my curiosity."

Recently, we conducted an informal e-mail survey of a small sample of some of the leading clinical research psychologists. We asked them to rank order their top three reasons for doing clinical research. They gave us a variety of answers but, for the most part, there was incredible consistency across the group. Their responses could be captured within the following themes:

1. Its rewarding nature

2. To satisfy scientific and intellectual curiosity

3. To inform clinical practice

Whether from our survey or in informal conversation with colleagues and graduate students, these three themes, or some variation on them, seem to dominate. So, what does this tell us? People get involved in clinical research because they find it rewarding in some way, it satisfies their curious nature, and it helps them in making important decisions in clinical practice. Below we discuss in more detail each of these themes.

It Is Rewarding

Based on response to our e-mail survey, it appears that clinical research can be rewarding in many ways. These include the rewards of interacting with stimulating and personable colleagues and students, being independent and having a flexible work schedule, professional accolades and incentives (e.g., invitations to speak at conferences, promotion), and contributing to the betterment of humankind. All of these rewards are important and all serve to motivate the clinical researcher. The most commonly expressed reward, however, is the sheer enjoyment that one gets from finding answers to important (or seemingly important) questions. So, in essence, the reward comes from satisfying curiosity, which, as noted above, was another common reason for doing research.

Satisfying Curiosity

Many years ago, a group of students who were finishing their undergraduate training and were planning to go to graduate school in psychology asked one of us (G. R. N.) how people chose one area of study over another. For example, why would one choose to pursue graduate training in experimental versus clinical psychology or vice versa? He didn't have a good answer so he suggested that the question would make a good group research project.

The students decided to see if two groups of psychologists—those who published mainly in clinical/applied journals, such as the *Journal of Consulting and Clinical Psychology*, and those who published mainly in experimental journals, such as the *Journal of Experimental Psychology*— differed in their interests, hobbies, and the like. The first group worked almost exclusively with people who had emotional disorders and were concerned with the assessment, description, and treatment of psychological disorders. The second group consisted of people who worked primarily with animals and were concerned with issues related to learning and brain function.

The students created a list of questions that required the respondent to choose between several options, such as, "In your free time, would you prefer to (a) read a book, (b) engage in a sports activity, (c) do house repairs," and so on. Other questions had to be answered on a 5-point scale, such as, "As a teenager did you enjoy science?: (a) not at all, (b) a little, (c) moderately, (d) quite a bit, and (e) very much." The questions were then given to faculty members in the psychology department for their evaluation. If a question received the endorsement of 75% of the professors, it was retained. The final list of questions was then sent to 50 well-known clinical researchers and 50 well-known basic researchers.

Approximately 60% of the people who received the questionnaires completed and returned them. The results were fascinating. Both groups of researchers were intensely curious people. They were fascinated by all sorts of things; but, the two groups differed in what fascinated them. The clinicians, as a group, were more "people focused." They spent more time reading biographies and watching people than did the basic researchers. The basic researchers, on the other hand, spent more time tinkering with gadgets. The main finding, however, was that the two groups loved to learn. The students believed that the researchers' curiosity was what started them doing research and what sustained their research.

Informing Clinical Practice

As clinicians, we are ultimately concerned with the well-being of our patients. It is not surprising, then, that much of our curiosity is about issues related to our patients' progress in treatment, specifically, and about the well-being of people, in general. As pointed out by several of the respondents to our e-mail survey, clinical researchers are often encouraged early in their career to ask questions about the status quo of the treatment strategies they are taught to administer. This is an approach that we strongly endorse. Always question what you are doing, why you are doing it, and whether it is the best approach.

Indeed, the current state of affairs in all health sciences is in flux as we learn more about various health conditions and the effects of various treatments on them. What is considered the best approach today might not be the state of the art tomorrow. Thus, we are always in a position to ask questions about why our treatments work for one person but not another, or whether a treatment that is effective for one condition might also work on a different set of symptoms.

Although somewhat arbitrary, and by no means mutually exclusive, we find it useful to categorize questions that inform clinical practice into several categories. These categories include questions that clarify an immediate concern, questions that test a specific idea, and questions that are meant to add to our current knowledge. Questions in all categories do the latter—add to the knowledge base—but the motivation behind the questions may be different.

Questions That Clarify a Concern

Many important clinical research projects are conducted to clarify a concern with some aspect of treatment. An excellent example of this is the early research done by Dr. Donald Klein, an eminent psychiatrist (Klein, 1964; Klein & Fink, 1962). In the 1960s, two new drugs were on the market—the benzodiazepines, such as Valium, and the tricyclic antidepressants, such as imipramine. Both were heralded as new wonder drugs. The benzodiazepines were thought to be a major breakthrough in treating anxiety neurosis and the tricyclics for treating depression. However, Klein and others found that not all people with anxiety neurosis improved with benzodiazepines. Klein reasoned that the tricyclics might be useful for treating some cases of anxiety because he had noted that when these drugs had been used with people who had other types of problems, but were also anxious, the anxiety decreased.

Klein gave benzodiazepines to half his patients with anxiety neurosis and a tricyclic antidepressant to the other half. He found that some patients in both drug groups improved markedly. However, those who improved after taking the tricyclics showed a very different symptom profile compared to those who improved after taking the benzodiazepines. Those who improved most with the tricyclics experienced rapid rushes of terror. Their hearts would race wildly and they would have trouble breathing. The patients who benefited most from the benzodiazepines did not have these rapid rushes of terror. Their anxiety would build more slowly and they had fewer intense physical symptoms.

This study did just what Klein hoped it would do—it helped clarify a major concern about why some, but not all, people responded to treatment. The problem was that anxiety neurosis was not one, but two disorders. As a consequence, anxiety neurosis was later divided into two separate disorders—Generalized Anxiety Disorder and Panic Disorder—which we now approach with quite different treatment regimens. The people with Generalized Anxiety Disorder were the ones who benefited most from the benzodiazepines, while those with Panic Disorder benefited more from the tricyclics.

Clarifying a concern serves a purpose beyond increasing your ability to understand and effectively treat your patients. Indeed, the results of studies that serve to improve clinical outcomes can also be used to market clinical practice. Insurance companies, the media, and the consumers of clinical services are increasingly becoming interested in the effectiveness of treatment services. So, being able to state your success rate and, importantly, having data (that was collected using sound methods and accurately and honestly interpreted) to back up your claim, will provide strong ammunition for responding to requests or, in some cases, demands in this regard. In this context, you might view the time you spend doing clinical research as an investment that will both improve your clinical skills and increase your practice volume.

To Test an Idea

Murray Sidman, in his excellent text *Tactics of Scientific Research* (Sidman, 1960) suggested that most research is done by simply asking a question of nature. These questions usually occur in one of two forms: "How come . . ." and "What if . . . ." The "how come" questions usually require descriptive answers and the "what if" questions typically require changes in the way something is being done. Whether you are a trainee or a practicing clinician, it is likely that you are asking one or both of these types of questions all of the time. Let's consider examples of each.

How Come?   An example of a "how come" question is, "How come there are many more women with agoraphobia when women are only slightly more likely than men to experience panic attacks, which many believe lead to the development of agoraphobia?" One possible answer to this question is that men are more likely to use alcohol to reduce the intensity of panic attacks and, as a result, develop an alcohol problem. If this hypothesis were true, maybe there would be a high prevalence of men with panic attacks in alcohol treatment centers. One of us (G. R. N.) and his students tested this hypothesis and found that, indeed, many people who abuse alcohol have frequent panic attacks and many of these people experienced panic attacks prior to abusing alcohol. However, panic attacks were more likely to be experienced by *female* alcoholics than by males (Cox, Norton, Dorward, & Fergusson, 1989; Malan, Norton, & Cox, 1993).

Although the original "how come" question was not answered, it did lead to a series of very interesting studies of people with Panic Disorder and alcohol abuse problems. For example, it was found that people with Panic Disorder and alcohol abuse, compared to those with either just an alcohol problem or just a Panic Disorder problem, were much more likely to attempt suicide (Norton, Rockman, Luy, & Marion, 1993). This, combined with the results of other studies, both within and outside of our group, have served to increase our understanding of people who present with these varying symptom profiles.

The outcome of the original study is not uncommon when doing research: We don't always find what we expect! But, if a study is done well, the results, positive or negative, are equally important. Although our notion that more men in alcohol treatment centers would present with panic attacks was not supported, other results were relevant. If we always proved what we thought, there would be no need to do research.

What If? As noted above, the "what if . . ." type of question usually involves changing or manipulating something. For example, one of us (G. J. G. A.) asked, "What if I had people with high scores on a scale that measures fear of anxiety symptoms hyperventilate? Would they show more anxiety than those with low scores on the test?" This reasoning was based on the observation that several important theories state that hyperventilation commonly occurs in some anxiety disorders. The sensations produced by hyperventilation are then seen as the onset of an anxiety attack. We found just what we expected. Those people who feared their symptoms of anxiety reported a greater number and severity of symptoms, such as a racing heart following a brief period of intentional hyperventilation, than did those low on the fear of anxiety symptoms (Asmundson, Norton, Wilson, & Sandler, 1994). Important, and unexpectedly, this occurred even though objective evidence, such as heart rates, did not differ between the two groups. This study changed (or manipulated) a simple thing—rate and depth of breathing—to see if it had different effects on people with different psychological characteristics.

Summary. The above examples depict simple studies designed to test fairly basic ideas stemming from observations, in the first instance, and theory, in the second, of clinical presentations of symptoms. Although based on different approaches, one descriptive and the other involving manipulation, both yielded answers and, through communication to a wider audience, led to unique and significant contributions to the literature.

To Add to Our Knowledge

In addition to any other motivating factors, clinical research, if done well, always serves to add to our knowledge base. This, as we hope is apparent above, is true whether clarifying a concern or testing an idea. We can add to our knowledge in many ways—by discovering something new, by confirming and extending previous findings, or by casting doubt on consensus or earlier findings.

New Discoveries. Although our knowledge about any segment of our lives usually grows by increments, sometimes discoveries are made that totally transform the way we think about things. In Chapter 1, we discussed several scientists whose discoveries had such an impact. Let's briefly revisit the research of Louis Pasteur. Pasteur made many seminal scientific contributions, ranging from the discovery of anaerobic life (i.e., life without oxygen) to methods of killing micro-organisms (i.e., pasteurization) and vaccinating against chicken pox, cholera, anthrax, and rabies. His contributions, considered by many to be cornerstones of modern medicine, were based on a systematic series of research projects over a 40-year period. Rarely, though, does a series of research projects revolutionize our thinking or clinical practice. The contributions are usually more modest.

Extending Knowledge.   Research is often done to see if what we know can be extended to new groups, new situations, or to improve what we are doing. In other words, this type of research begins with a fairly well-established phenomenon and extends it. For example, as we discussed above, Klein and others have established that many people with Panic Disorder respond well to the tricyclic antidepressant, imipramine. Good responders show a marked reduction in the number and frequency of panic attacks, a reduction in overall anxiety, and an increased ability to go places and do things.

If this drug works well for people with Panic Disorder, it might also work well with other anxiety disorders that have similar presentations. Panic Disorder and Social Anxiety Disorder have many similarities. People with both disorders avoid social activities, experience panic attacks, and have similar co-occurring problems such as depression. Their avoidance of social situations is for different reasons; however, the similarities are marked enough that it would be interesting to see if the conditions both respond to the same medication.

The results of several studies agree—people with Social Anxiety Disorder don't respond very well to some of the medications that are useful for people with Panic Disorder (Liebowitz et al., 1992). Even though the results of these studies were negative, they added to our knowledge by showing that, despite being similar in some ways, Panic Disorder and Social Anxiety Disorder differ in their response to medications.

Challenging Current Understanding.   Researchers may also conduct studies to challenge the current understanding of a condition, an assessment tool or strategy, or an approach to treatment. For example, consider the observation that depression is associated with many painful health conditions, such as multiple sclerosis or low back pain. Quite often, the depressive symptoms overlap considerably with the physical symptoms, making it hard to distinguish the primary source of the symptom. Are sleep difficulties and work inhibition expressions of depression, physical condition, or both?

Despite this type of ambiguity, clinicians and researchers have traditionally assessed depression in patients with physical conditions by giving and scoring measures of depression in the same way they would do so in any other group. A series of recent studies suggests, however, that the typical way of scoring a depression measure may artificially inflate the depression score in patients with physical conditions by including symptoms that are endorsed but that are not actually a result of depression. As a result, there is a healthy empirical debate ongoing in the literature as to whether revised (e.g., Chibnall & Tait, 1994; Mohr et al., 1997) or traditional scoring should be used (e.g., Aikens et al., 1999). Ultimately, this debate over assessment strategy may lead to improved understanding of the relationship between depression and painful health conditions, the mechanisms that influence that relationship, and the most appropriate target for intervention.

Summary.   Most published clinical research adds to our knowledge base by building on or challenging the current state of the art. Fewer contributions are related to new discoveries. This is not to say, though, that modest contributions are not important. Indeed, it is these modest contributions, over time and in response to some aspect of the existing literature, that lead to advances in our knowledge and application of it to the betterment of our patients.

So, Why Should You Do Research?

We have presented a number of reasons why some of the leading clinical research psychologists do research—it is rewarding, it satisfies their inherent curiosity, and it informs and guides their clinical practice. Though these capture some of the general themes, all expressed their reasons in somewhat different ways and with different priorities. Why should you do clinical research? If you do get involved, you, too, will have your own reasons. For those of you pursuing interests in an academic research environment the flexible work schedule, opportunities to interact with intelligent people, and the professional accolades may be particularly relevant. On the other hand, those of you attempting to fit research into a tight schedule of clinical duties may rank improved clinical practice and profile as the primary reason. Whatever your reasons, and whether you aspire toward a more academic or more clinical career path, we do hope that the information in this chapter has stimulated your enthusiasm to make research part of your regular activities. And, now that we have you enthused, we will turn attention to sources of research ideas.

References

Aikens, J. E., Reinecke, M. A., Pliskin, N. H., Fischer, J. S., Wiebe, J. S., McCracken, L. M., & Taylor, J. L. (1999). Assessing depressive symptoms in multiple sclerosis: Is it necessary to omit items from the original Beck Depression Inventory? *Journal of Behavioral Medicine, 22,* 127–142.

Asmundson, G. J. G., Norton, G. R., Wilson, K. H., & Sandler, L. S. (1994). Subjective symptoms and cardiac reactivity to brief hyperventilation in individuals with high anxiety sensitivity. *Behaviour Research and Therapy, 32,* 237–241.

Chibnall, J. T., & Tait, R. C. (1994). The short form of the Beck Depression Inventory: Validity issues with chronic pain patients. *The Clinical Journal of Pain, 10,* 261–266.

Cox, B. J., Norton, G. R., Dorward, J., & Fergusson, P. A. (1989). The relationship between panic attacks and chemical dependencies. *Addictive Behaviors, 14,* 53–60.

Klein, D. F. (1964). Delineation of two drug-responsive anxiety syndromes. *Psychopharmacologia, 5,* 397–408.

Klein, D. F., & Fink, M. (1962). Psychiatric reaction patterns to imipramine. *American Journal of Psychiatry, 119,* 432–438.

Liebowitz, M. R., Schneier, F., Campeas, R., Hollander, E., Hatterer, J., Fyer, A., Gorman, J., Papp, L., Davies, S., Gully, R., & Klein, D. F. (1992). Phenelzine vs atenolol in social phobia. A placebo-controlled comparison. *Archives of General Psychiatry, 49,* 290–300.

Malan, J. R., Norton, G. R., & Cox, B. J. (1993). Panic attacks and alcoholism: Primacy and frequency of attacks. *Alcoholism Treatment Quarterly, 10,* 95–105.

Mohr, D. C., Goodkin, D. E., Likosky, W., Beutler, L., Gatto, N., & Langan, M. K. (1997). Identification of Beck Depression Inventory items related to multiple sclerosis. *Journal of Behavioral Medicine, 20,* 407–414.

Norton G. R., Rockman, G. E., Luy, B., & Marion, T. (1993). Suicide, chemical abuse, and panic attacks: A preliminary report. *Behaviour Research and Therapy, 31,* 37–40.

Sidman, M. (1960). *Tactics of scientific research.* New York: Basic Books.

3

Generating Worthwhile Research Ideas and Setting an Action Plan

How can you generate research ideas and how do you know if a research idea is a good one? These are critical questions. In our experience, clinicians and students have no shortage of ideas that might be subjected to the research method. But, whether you are asking it of your own idea or of one that you are hearing or reading about, the question of whether an idea is good is particularly important.

Also important is the nature of the idea. Many ideas are expressed as questions that are exploratory in nature. For example, you might ask, "What proportion of the people who have had a stroke become depressed in the months immediately following their stroke?" or "Is there a relationship between drug preferences and personality characteristics and, if so, does it have any bearing on addiction?" These questions are similar in many ways to the "how come" questions discussed in Chapter 2. The answers to these questions often come from preliminary studies that are meant to shed light on the matter by providing basic, simple data.

Other ideas are stated as a prediction, or an *hypothesis,* that is either proved or disproved by the research. For example, you might predict that, "If people who are socially anxious are treated with a combination of psychotherapy and medication, then they will have larger reduction in their anxiety compared to those treated with either psychotherapy or medication alone." Ideas that are stated as predictions are similar to the "what if" questions discussed in Chapter 2 and typically come after a rudimentary, or basic understanding of an issue is at hand. That is, we usually start testing predictions after many of the exploratory questions have been answered.

In this chapter we consider some common sources of ideas. These sources include intuition, theory, and previous research. As well, we will discuss criteria that can be used to determine the value of your idea and whether you should pursue researching it. Finally, we will outline the actions that need to be taken once you have made the decision to start a research project.

Whatever the source of your idea—intuition, theory, or previous research—a word of caution is warranted. *Keep it simple!* Do not try to answer too many questions, hypotheses, or both within the same study. This common mistake, often made by many beginning researchers, can lead to difficulty in completing the overly complex project, frustration, and disillusionment with the whole process. This caution also applies to more seasoned veterans of clinical research, although, as you become more experienced, you should be able to increase complexity in a manner that is manageable.

Sources of Research Ideas

Most of you already have an abundance of ideas that you could test using research methods. Still, it is important to consider various sources of ideas in some depth. By doing so you may gain insight into important aspects of your idea that might otherwise be overlooked. The most common sources include intuition, theory, and previous research.

Intuition

Intuition is, quite simply, a feeling that something should be a certain way—a hunch. It may be a product of common sense, your personal views and experiences, or both. In the history of science there are multiple examples of landmark theoretical and practical advances that have resulted from hunches. Some of the best-known examples are within the domain of physics, where the intuitive ideas of Newton and Einstein led to a general understanding of gravity and to the theory of relativity, respectively. In both cases, these scientists relied on their intuition to explain their observations of naturally occurring events. There are also numerous examples within the medical and social sciences. For example, penicillin and the principles of classical conditioning were generated directly from intuitive explanations of observed phenomena.

We would be surprised if you have not used intuition to explain, or at least try to explain, unique clinical situations that you have encountered. In doing so it is likely that you have developed, and perhaps discussed with colleagues, a number of ideas that might serve to shed light on the situation at hand. Some of these hunches may already have been tested by others, in which case you might compare your thoughts to existing empirical evidence. In other cases, your hunch may be one that addresses an issue that is unique and previously untested.

Some intuitive ideas may be amenable to systematic evaluation, and some not. In the case where you have a seemingly unique idea that you want to evaluate, there are a couple of criteria that should be met. First, as noted above, you should see if another researcher has already published data that might support your hunch. Second, your idea should be feasible to evaluate. Finally, if you want to evaluate a hunch that involves manipulation (or, is a "what if" question), it must be expressed in a way that is falsifiable. That is, you must be able to disprove it (for an excellent and detailed discussion see Stanovich, 1998). The intuitive ideas of Newton, Einstein, Fleming, and Pavlov were both feasible to test and falsifiable. There are many instances, however, where this was not the case. For example, when an epidemic of yellow fever hit Philadelphia in the late 1700s, Benjamin Rush, an eminent doctor in the city at the time, attributed all cases of improved health to efficacy of his yellow fever treatment and all cases of death to disease severity (Eisenberg, 1977). His idea was not stated in a falsifiable manner; so, no matter the outcome, he could explain it in a way that supported his contention of the effectiveness of his treatment—simply stated, if a patient got better it was due to the treatment, but if the patient died it was because the disease had progressed to too severe a state. Collectively, these three criteria—have previous studies addressed the idea, is it feasible, and is it falsifiable—are critical to the evaluation of research ideas, regardless of their source.

Theory

Some clinical researchers believe that most research ideas (except, perhaps, for those relating to practical issues such as cost-effectiveness) should be rooted in theory. Why do they believe this? The answer has to do with the nature of theory. A theory, in general, is an organized set of assumptions, propositions, or principles that serves to provide a parsimonious account of existing data from which new ideas can be deduced. So, a theory is based on data and can be used to generate ideas that, through testing, can spawn new data. These new data may then fit the theory, by agreeing with its assumptions, propositions, or principles, or they may not. In the latter case, modification to the theory may be warranted. Ideas that are rooted in theory have, by definition, a context in which to be understood, and the outcomes of testing those ideas can themselves influence that context.

Previous Research

Previous research is an invaluable source of research ideas. This may already be apparent from our discussion in Chapter 2. There we noted that two important reasons for doing research were to extend or challenge existing knowledge that, of course, is based on previous research. Your ideas, thus, may come from reading the previous literature in your area of interest and noting ways to extend it, challenging its assumptions, or addressing shortcomings in the methods or statistics used. In many cases, researchers will conclude their papers with a list of ideas that need to be addressed by future research. Some of these lists are more specific and detailed than others; but, regardless, these are excellent sources for feasible and important research ideas.

We have not yet considered replication of previous research findings, another source of research ideas, in any detail. Replication simply means trying to find the same results as another researcher using the same (or similar) participants, methods, and analyses. Let's consider an example that illustrates the process of replication and underscores its importance. In Chapter 10, we provide basic information on the use of statistics in analyzing your data but, for the purposes of this example, the following statistical information is important. When we use statistics to compare scores of two or more groups, we are determining if the differences in scores between the groups are meaningful. Are the scores on a measure of depression for the people we encourage to engage in volunteer work significantly lower at the end of treatment compared to those whom we didn't encourage to engage in volunteer work? To test this, we use an estimate of the likelihood that the differences (if there are differences) are due to chance. Our estimate of probability is the p value. It has become somewhat of a convention to state that if the p value is less than .05, the differences between our group scores are meaningful.

The p value tells us that the likelihood of the differences having occurred by chance are fewer than five times in one hundred. In other words, we can be reasonably sure that our observed differences are due to real differences between the groups. However, there still are five chances in one hundred that the differences may be due to chance factors.

One of the authors (G. R. N.) discovered this in a very real way when he was doing research for his Ph.D. dissertation. He was attempting to extend some research that demonstrated that if you cannulate (i.e., insert into the body through a tube) certain chemicals into the hypothalamus of a rat, you could make a hungry rat stop feeding. Other chemicals were supposed to make a sated rat hungry. Previously published research showed these effects very clearly. However, when G. R. N. attempted to replicate these effects, he couldn't. He went so far as to contact the original researcher and get his chemicals and his cannula. He still couldn't replicate the effects.

Later, the original researcher attempted to replicate his earlier findings and couldn't. Why? It appears that the effects were due to chance or to other uncontrolled factors. If G. R. N. and the original researcher had not attempted to replicate these effects, other researchers would have continued to believe that eating behavior could easily be manipulated by simply putting certain chemicals into the hypothalamus of a rat.

There are many examples of how researchers have failed to replicate what appeared to be meaningful research findings. In other instances, findings are consistently replicated. Through this important process, our knowledge progresses. We test and retest the same, or variations on the same, research ideas. Although not necessary, this process often occurs in the context of theory.

Is the Idea Worth Investing In?

Now you have an idea. Good! This is a fundamental step. But, it is only the start. You now have to determine whether your idea is worth developing and systematically evaluating. We like to think that if any research idea is well thought out, it is worth investing in. That said, let's look at some questions you should ask yourself in thinking through your idea:

1. Why do I want to do research?

2. What will I gain by doing research on this idea?

3. What will my idea contribute to our understanding of the condition I am interested in?

4. Do I have the time and resources to do research on this idea?

Questions 1 and 2

The first and second questions are similar in some ways and both relate closely to our Chapter 2 discussion of why people get involved in clinical research. The question of why you want to do research is, however, a fundamental one that needs to be considered carefully. It asks for your basic motivation for doing research. This motivation might include things you will gain from doing research, such as credit toward your degree, promotion, or social reinforcement from colleagues. But, for a researcher interested in clinical phenomena, it should *definitely* involve basic issues of curiosity regarding basic or practical clinical issues. In an ideal world, this is probably the purest motivation for doing clinical research. If this is one of your reasons, then we encourage you to proceed with your research.

Now, let's take a closer look at the second question, "What will I gain by doing research on this idea?" It is not trivial. Although research should always be based on curiosity, other reasons may be important. For example, many universities require publications and conference presentations for promotion from one rank to another. Often promotion is associated with salary. This may seem like a crass reason for doing research, but another way of thinking about it is to assume that research is part of your job description.

You also may do research as an opportunity to travel to conferences. Indeed, some institutions are more likely to fund trips to conferences if you are presenting at the conference. Attending conferences has many advantages. First, it gives you an opportunity to present your ideas and research to a learned group of peers. Their feedback can be very reinforcing and encourage additional research ideas. Second, you will have opportunities to learn about others' research and ideas. These ideas could have an important impact on your clinical work, as well as your future research projects. Third, since most clinically oriented conferences also offer clinical workshops, attending the conference can furnish an opportunity to get clinical training from the leaders in the area who, otherwise, may never visit your institution. Finally, attending conferences is a great opportunity to visit with friends and colleagues and to meet new people. This is especially important for novice researchers. They can make important connections with others that can affect later job opportunities, participation in future conferences or work groups, and collaborative clinical research.

Finally, most people who do research derive great pleasure from seeing their name on a publication or conference presentation. We know many researchers who have published many articles who are, nevertheless, still thrilled at seeing their name on a publication (ourselves included).

Research is not always inherently fun to do. It can, in some cases, take up time that you may feel you should devote to other aspects of your life (whether these are career related or not). Thus, although most of us would like to be able to do research simply because of curiosity, sometimes we need other reasons such as promotion or prestige to justify our efforts. In other words, sometimes we need to find additional reinforcers to support our efforts. When they occur, doing research becomes much more fun.

Question 3

The third question, "What will my idea contribute to our understanding of the condition I am interested in?" is also very important. It is, however, one that is often not easy to answer in advance of systematically evaluating your idea. Your idea may end up contributing very little or, ideally, it may prove extremely significant.

Many good ideas have not been studied because we tend to trivialize them. We might think they are silly or that others would have already researched the idea. This is unfortunate and, as a result of this type of thinking (a form of catastrophizing, it seems), good ideas are often put aside and don't get studied. Yet because many of our most interesting ideas for research are initially based on problems that arise from situations that occur in our daily activities, they should not be automatically trivialized.

Many patients in our clinical settings may not respond as the textbooks tell us they should. As a result, we might come up with an idea that might improve treatment for patients with a particular problem. If we can conceptualize a new way of treating this problem, we have the germ of a potentially good research idea. Illustration 3.1 gives several examples of ideas from clinical situations that are worth researching.

Question 4

Do I have time? Do I have resources? We have discussed some of the issues relevant to these questions in Chapter 1. These are very real issues. Fortunately, some research projects require few resources beyond time for things like planning and writing. Other projects may require more extensive resources such as funding, research assistants, and special equipment.

Money is necessary to many projects. You may need to buy supplies, expertise, research assistants, and, in some cases, time. Unfortunately, grant money to support research can be very difficult to obtain. Many of the major granting councils have limited funds, usually require a good publication track record along with a detailed proposal, and are very selective in the projects they fund. This sounds a bit discouraging. Fortunately, if you are just getting started with research, there are often other sources of funding that you may access. Hospitals, clinics, and universities often have start-up funds to support research. If you are at one of these institutions, you should contact your director of research for information on how to apply for in-house funding.

Illustration 3.1.   Ideas Worth Researching

---

1. *Your observations are inconsistent with what you have read or heard.* Many studies using both medications and psychotherapy have been done on "pure" samples of people who have just one problem. In real life, we rarely see "pure" problems. For example, most people who have panic disorder also have other anxiety or mood disorders. You may have noticed that people with complex problems don't respond to treatment in the same way as described in the literature or by the information you have received from the drug companies. Maybe complex problems require a different approach.

2. *Your idea may provide a better way of understanding or treating a problem.* The history of psychology and psychiatry is filled with advances in our understanding and treatment of psychological disorders. We are sure that we haven't found the final answers for describing, assessing, and treating disorders. For example, look at the changes that have been made in the diagnostic criteria for various disorders in recent editions of the *Diagnostic and Statistical Manual of Mental Disorders* (American Psychiatric Association, 1986, 1990, 1994, 2000). Similarly, if we compare treatment procedures described in textbooks in the 1980s with current texts, we can see that treatments for many disorders have changed rather markedly. Your ideas may improve on our understanding of the nature and treatment of mental and other disorders.

3. *Your idea may simply be an interesting "what if" question.* This type of question is often specific to a current problem you are trying to solve. For example, one of the authors recently was having difficulty treating a young woman who had a severe "vomit phobia." She was both very afraid that she would vomit and afraid of seeing another person vomit. He knew that exposure therapy would be helpful, but how could he expose her to vomiting conditions without actually inducing vomiting, a procedure he found inappropriate. He wondered what would happen if he had her watch her boyfriend pretend to vomit soup he had filled his mouth with? He suggested the idea to his client and she agreed to do it. It worked very well. She even practiced the pretend vomiting on several occasions. As a result, she began feeling that, although she would prefer not to vomit, it would be tolerable if she did.

Many larger communities, states, and provinces also have funding agencies that you may be able to access. The best ways to obtain information about these agencies is either to contact the director of your nearest large university and ask for information on local funding agencies, or go on the Web. We have found that most granting agencies have Web sites that clearly explain their criteria for providing grants and how to apply for their grants. A convenient search term is "research grants." This often requires you to step through many links until you find granting agencies that are appropriate to your needs. However, you will likely be surprised at how many granting agencies there are.

You may also wish to consider private or charitable organizations. Many of these provide research funding. Private agencies can also be reached by using the Web. These often provide surprisingly good sources for support of specialized projects. For example, if you were interested in the effects of cardiovascular fitness on mood states, you might wish to contact a local heart disease charity.

The Action Plan

Once you have decided to invest your time and energy into a specific research project, you need to establish an action plan. The action plan is, quite simply, a series of steps that you need to take in order get the research ball rolling and to keep it rolling. These steps, listed below and in the Action Plan Checklist provided in Illustration 3.2, include the following:

1. Reviewing the existing literature

2. Writing a research proposal (Chapter 5)

3. Ensuring the project complies with ethical standards (see Chapter 6)

4. Determining if you have adequate resources for collecting meaningful data (Chapters 7, 8, and 9)

5. Determining if you have the necessary data analytic and technical skills to do the project (Chapter 10)

6. Preparing a plan for communicating your findings (Chapters 11 and 12)

These are essential steps in any research plan. It is preferable to address all steps before you begin collecting your data. However, this is not always possible. We strongly recommend that you *always* do your best to complete Steps 1 through 4 *before* you begin. If you are conducting research in the context of your own clinical practice, a fully developed proposal may not be necessary. But, nevertheless, the written proposal is a good idea because, even if brief, it will serve to strengthen your understanding of the issue at hand, your grasp on the pertinent details, and to guide you as the project progresses. Below we consider the *first part* of Step 1, gathering pertinent articles from the existing literature for review. The rest of the book is devoted to the details of the remaining steps.

Illustration 3.2.   The Action Plan Checklist

- Try your research ideas out on your peers or mentor and get feedback.

- Review the existing literature using search databases. It may be a good idea to search more than one database to ensure that you don't limit the focus of your review—someone else may have already studied your problem, but in a different discipline.

- Based on discussion and results of your literature search, and careful consideration of your interests, time, and available resources, draft a research proposal. Consider applying for grant funding for your project.

- Submit an application for ethical approval of your research study to the appropriate institution(s), such as a hospital or university.

- Determine if you have adequate knowledge/resources for analyzing your data. You may want to consider consulting with others who have expertise with statistics or other data analyses methods (i.e., qualitative) pertinent to your research.

- Collect, analyze, and interpret your data.

- Discuss your findings with your peers or mentor, asking for critical feedback. Doing so will ensure that you haven't missed something significant in your interpretation and may provide you with a broader perspective.

- Prepare and present your research for conference presentation and/or submit a manuscript to an appropriate journal for publication consideration.

Gathering Articles From the Literature

You need to be aware of other people's research before you start your own. The easiest way to do this is by (a) gathering the pertinent existing literature on the topic you are interested in and then (b) reviewing and critically evaluating it. Fortunately, gathering pertinent literature is fairly easy to do. There are a number electronic databases that provide abstracts of previously published research. These databases are usually very easy to access and are very user-friendly. Most university and hospital libraries have computers from which you can gain access. Sometimes you can even access the databases from your home or work computer. For example, you can search the medical database described below for free by logging on to Medscape, an Internet site devoted to various aspects of medicine, at www.medscape.com. You might also search the electronic databases of the American Psychological Association.

We provide a brief description of the two databases that are commonly used by clinical researchers in psychology and medicine—PsycLit and Medline. As well, we provide a brief introduction to searching for articles on PsycLit and Medline.

PsycLit

PsycLit is a database owned and operated by the American Psychological Association. PsycLit annually references more than 55,000 journal articles published in approximately 1,300 international journals. The abstracts in PsycLit come from journals in all fields of psychology and related disciplines. This can sometimes be both an advantage and a disadvantage. The advantage is that you will be able to obtain abstracts published by researchers from very different backgrounds. For example, you may find abstracts on suicide published by researchers with backgrounds in social psychology, personality, and clinical psychology to name but a few. People with different backgrounds often have very different perspectives and ask very different, but equally intriguing, research questions. This diversity of questions and their answers may provide you with a much clearer picture of the problem you are interested in than what might come from people from just one area of expertise. The disadvantage is that your search will obtain many abstracts that are not relevant to your interests, and these will need to be *weeded* out.

Medline

Medline is a medical database published by the United States National Library of Medicine. It annually abstracts approximately 400,000 articles published in more than 3,600 international journals. The abstracts in Medline cover all areas of medicine and related disciplines. There is some overlap between the abstracts in PsycLit and Medline. As a general rule, the abstracts in Medline are more likely to address biological and medical issues compared to PsycLit. For example, you are much more likely to find articles on pharmacotherapy in Medline than you are in PsycLit. PsycLit, however, would be more likely to provide abstracts of articles where the focus is on basic psychological processes, such as cognition.

Searching

Both of these databases use "key word" search strategies. If, for example, you were interested in finding out what articles had been published on the relationship between suicide and fingernail biting, you would enter the terms *suicide* and *fingernail biting* as key words. When these key words are entered into the computer, the program will search all of the articles in the database for those two sets of key words. The computer would then provide you with the total number of abstracts in which the key words appear.

In order to make your search more specific, you can string key words together. Instead of just searching the key word *suicide* and then *fingernail biting,* you could string them together by entering both terms separated by the word *and.* In fact, you can string several terms together to restrict your search even more precisely. When we searched for "suicide and fingernail biting," there were no articles in PsycLit and five in Medline.

Because there are such a large number of abstracts that have been archived in the databases, you may be required to inform the computer program of the time frame you wish to search. For example, you may wish to start out by looking only at articles that have been published in the past 5 years. Given the small number of articles on "suicide and nail biting," this was not necessary. However, in the case of "suicide and depression," for which there were 1,629 articles listed in Medline between 1966 and 2000, setting limits would be advised.

Once you have determined the number of abstracts in which the key word appears, you can view each of the abstracts to determine if it is relevant to your interests. If an abstract is of interest, you can instruct the computer program to "save" the abstract for you. After you have selected the abstracts of interest you can either download them to disk or print them.

Although the computer programs for both PsycLit and Medline provide very clear instructions for their use, most libraries that have the databases have knowledgeable librarians who can provide you with help. These and other similar databases have made reviewing the literature very easy. With your list of relevant abstracts in hand you can now gather together the corresponding research articles.

Summary

The purpose of this chapter was to consider several good sources of research ideas—intuition, theory, and previous research—and criteria for determining whether you want to immerse yourself in an actual research project. Do you have the time? Do you have the resources? Will you learn something that might inform your clinical practice? We also looked at the steps necessary in seeing the project through to fruition—the action plan—and, importantly, the first part of the first step of reviewing the literature—gathering relevant articles from the published literature. Now, with these articles in hand, it's time get down to the *second part* of the literature review process. Yes, it's time to read those articles! But, reading research articles is different from reading the newspaper or your favorite fiction novel. In the next chapter we provide a primer on reading and critically evaluating research articles.

References

Eisenberg, L. (1977). The social imperatives of medical research. *Science, 198,* 1105–1110.

Stanovich, K. E. (1998). *How to think straight about psychology* (5th ed.). New York: Addison Wesley Longman.

4

How to Read and Critically Evaluate Research Articles

R esearch can be communicated in a number of formats. The most
accessible is the journal article. Conference symposia and poster
presentations are also common, but attendance at these is not always feasible.
In Part 3 we discuss how to prepare research information for dissemination
in these various forms. Regardless of the communication format, you need
to be able to make sense of the research and to evaluate it critically if you
are to benefit from it. Here we focus on evaluating research articles; however,
many of the same principles apply to conference presentations (and, famili-
arizing yourself with the tips for effective verbal and poster presentations
presented in Chapter 11 will further equip you).

There are several excellent sources of information about the ways in
which you might go about critically evaluating research presentations, written or otherwise. A 1996 book by Ellen R. Girden, titled *Evaluating
Research Articles: From Start to Finish,* is dedicated to this process, as are
the chapters of some edited books (e.g., Bellack & Hersen, 1984; Oleson &
Arkin, 1996). As well, a few journal editors have published article review
checklists that are based on feedback from reviewers (Campion, 1993) and
guides for assessing research article content from the reviewer and contribu-
tor perspectives (e.g., Eysenck & Eysenck, 1992; Maher, 1978).

There are probably as many approaches to reviewing articles with a critical eye as there are people who review articles. Some approaches may be
more efficient than others, but most important is understanding what basic
points to consider in the evaluation process. Once you understand what
needs to be considered, you will develop your own style of reviewing.

It is likely that you have already had many opportunities to read published research articles. The important question is, therefore, not whether you are reading, but *how* you are reading. What is the best strategy for reading and evaluating research articles? The model we recommend involves progressing through a series of specific steps that are geared toward teasing out the most important information from the various sections of a research article. This model has proven quite effective in getting our students to think critically about the articles they read.

Our model can be challenging at first, and at times it can appear intimidating to those not familiar with the process of critical reading. But we are very confident that, given a little patience and practice, as well as some familiarity with the topics discussed in Part 2 of this book, this strategy will improve your proficiency in reading and critically evaluating a research article. Let's take a look at the steps involved.

Getting Started

Even at an advanced stage of training, and thereafter, there are many people who, unfortunately, do not take full advantage of the information provided in a research article. A surprising number of students (and, in many cases, professionals) read the Introduction, none or only parts of the Method, and skip right to the Discussion for a summary of the study and its findings. Admittedly, this strategy is quick. It does not, however, allow you to fully and critically evaluate the strengths, weaknesses, and limitations of a research project. It may even leave you with a misunderstanding of the article and, in many cases, nothing more than ideas based on speculation about observed results. Surely, journal editors or reviewers would be considered neglectful if they read articles in this way. You, as well, should avoid adopting this as your sole strategy *at all costs* (which is mostly the time it takes you to read the article carefully).

Let's look at an example to illustrate how erroneous conclusions can be drawn on the basis of reading only select portions of an article. A few years ago, we conducted a study to see if a predisposition to be fearful was predictive of fear of pain and escape/avoidance behavior in people with chronic pain (Asmundson & Taylor, 1996). We found this to be the case and concluded, "The results of the present study have an important clinical implication. They suggest that interventions that reduce [the predisposition] will also reduce pain-related fear and escape/avoidance" (p. 585). If a person read the entire article, it would be clear that the conclusions regarding usefulness of this treatment approach were speculative and required further investigation. If, on the other hand, the person read only the discussion or its concluding remarks, it is possible that an erroneous conclusion might be drawn—one that assumed we had actually tested and found these treatments to be effective when, in fact, we did not even test this.

Were we wrong to speculate about treatment efficacy? No, not in this case. Our speculation stemmed directly from our findings and, thus, was warranted. It would, however, have been an error for us to have drawn conclusions about things that did not follow directly from our findings. It would also be an error on the part of a reader of our article to conclude that our speculation was anything more than that.

It is important to keep in mind throughout your reading that just because an idea is published does not mean that it cannot be criticized. Indeed, the scientific peer review process—the process by which articles are written, submitted to a journal, reviewed by fellow researchers, and ultimately accepted for publication or otherwise turned down and not published—has itself been criticized. There is a whole literature on the pros and cons of scientific peer review that provides rather intriguing, and sometimes empirically based, insights into the process. If you are interested in exploring this further, we recommend that you read the commentary of Epstein (1995) as well as responses to it in subsequent issues of *American Psychologist* and related empirical articles (e.g., Goldbeck-Wood, 1999; van Rooyen, Godlee, Evans, Black, & Smith, 1999).

Regardless of its pros and cons, the scientific peer review process is based on the principle of critical evaluation. This is not to say that the sole focus is on weaknesses and limitations. Rather, positive and negative features of the research, as presented in the research article, should be equally recognized and considered. We now discuss the steps of this process in a manner that should allow you to become proficient at it and apply it in your own reading.

Step 1: The Initial Read

In order to evaluate critically a research article—to consider its negative as well as positive features—it is usually necessary to read it more than once. This, of course, implies that you have a specific research article that you want or need to read. (If copying the article, be certain that you also copy the reference section. It is very important but something that is often forgotten in the process.) A technique that we have found helpful is to read an article carefully in its entirety, without taking too much time for being critical or taking notes, and then to put it away for a day or two. During this "break" from the article, you may find it helpful to scan through some

Illustration 4.1. Types of Articles

Type	Content
Empirical	Contains information related to an original research investigation conducted by the authors. New findings are presented.
Review	Provides a review and synthesis of previous research on a specific topic within a research area. In addition to providing details of previous research conclusions about progress, clinical implications and directions for future research in the area are often offered.
Clinical	Most often provides details pertaining to assessment, diagnosis, and treatment issues of a case or series of cases.
Book chapter	Like the review article, typically contains a review and synthesis of previous research in a given area. In some cases, authors also present reanalyses of previously reported data or new data.

review articles or books (see Illustration 4.1) in order get a general and current understanding of the area or topic you are reading about.

Oleson and Arkin (1996) suggest two other approaches that you might find useful in getting an initial "feel" for the article. The first is to read the abstract, followed by the first paragraph of the introduction, the last paragraph of the discussion, and then a general scanning of all other sections. The second is to read the abstract followed by the first sentence of every paragraph. Again, this could be followed by a scan of relevant review articles and books.

Before proceeding to Step 2 ask yourself whether the article is worth spending your time on. This is particularly important when doing background reading relevant to your research or clinical endeavors when time is at a premium. You don't want to waste time on a marginally relevant study! You can make this determination by asking questions like, "Is the specific topic relevant?" "Does some aspect of the study hold implications for my research?" and "Do the authors address and comment on an assessment or treatment issue that holds implications for what I am doing?" If the answer to these sorts of questions is "No," then you may want to find another article before proceeding to Step 2.

Step 2: The Second Read

Subsequent to this initial read, the article can be reread with the particular intent of identifying its strengths, weaknesses, and limitations. By having previously read the article, or parts of it, you will have a general understanding of "what the article is about and what conclusions it offers," and you can focus on the more critical issues. The number of times the article needs to be reread depends on a number of factors, including its complexity and your familiarity with the area.

When reading an article you may wish to consider the purpose of each of the sections and the type of information that can be derived. On the second reading, keep critical issues in mind. Now is the time to make detailed notes. Below, we provide a summary of the type of information that is typical of the abstract, introduction, method, results, and discussion sections of an article.

Abstract

The abstract should provide a brief summary of the purpose and/or hypothesis of the study, the methodology, the nature of the results (i.e., did they support the hypothesis), and the implications of the results. In some cases, researchers present summary statistics related to the primary findings. When you are glancing through a journal or searching electronic databases such as PsycLit or Medline (see Chapter 3), the abstract is often the only part of a research article that you will see. Therefore, the abstract should be informative enough to give you an idea of whether you want to read (or can benefit from reading) the entire article. In this sense, the abstract is one of the most important parts of the anatomy of a research article.

Introduction

It is necessary to fully understand the information presented in the Introduction because it tells (or should tell) you

- how the researchers came up with their question/hypothesis
- why the question/hypothesis is important (the rationale)
- what the current state of knowledge is regarding the question/hypothesis
- why the proposed method is appropriate to addressing the question/hypothesis (an excellent resource is the *Handbook of Research Methods in Clinical Psychology* [Kendall, Butcher, & Holmbeck, 1999])

Understanding the Introduction is not always easy and may depend on the nature and complexity of the information provided. Often an article is written primarily for other "experts" within a particular field of study. Thus, it may be necessary to read some of the other articles that the researchers refer to (thus the importance of copying the reference section when you copy the article), to look up unfamiliar terms, or both.

When critiquing the introduction, it is helpful to consider the following questions:

- Is the research question/hypothesis important or trivial?
- Is the question/hypothesis logically based in theory and/or on previous observations?
- Is this theory and related research presented and fairly critiqued?
- Would alternative theories make the same prediction?
- Is the purpose of the research clearly stated?
- Is the overall rationale for the research sound?
- Do the authors propose a method appropriate to addressing the purpose of the research?
- Does the proposed research provide a good test of the prediction?
- Could a different approach be used?

Method

The Method section describes the basic characteristics of the research participants, what was done to the participants (or what they were required to do), and what measures were used. The Method section should be reasonably simple to understand and should provide a "recipe" for you to conduct an identical study if you wish. This is a good test of whether the Method section contains sufficient information—if you wanted to, could you go about conducting the study based on the information provided? If the answer is "yes" or "probably," excellent! If the answer is "unlikely" or "no," then important information is likely to be missing.

Before you proceed to the Results section you should have a good understanding of

- who the participants were and how they were selected
- what was done to them
- the tasks/actions that they performed
- the general design of the investigation

Typically, this information will be found in various subsections of the Method section. These generally include Subjects/Participants, Procedure, and Design subsections. Below we provide a list of points to consider in critiquing each of these. (This is where things can start to get intimidating and from whence the urge to *skip* to the Discussion comes. This is also where the guidance of a mentor, if available, or reference to Part 2 of this book can be helpful).

Critiquing Subjects/Participants Section.   This section should, at minimum, describe the participants (some writers and journals use the term *subjects* but, given current trends in psychology, *participants* has become the preferred term and we will use it here). First, factors such as average age, average level of education, sex distribution, and related demographic information should be provided. Second, clinical characteristics should be described. For example, in the case of people with chronic pain these might include factors such as duration, location, and severity of pain. Finally, in cases where there are multiple groups, this section should clearly and specifically detail how participants were assigned to the groups, whether an attempt was made to match the groups (e.g., for age, level of education, socio-economic status), and whether groups differ significantly on demographic or clinical characteristics. In the latter case, some researchers choose to put this information in the Results section. However, regardless of placement in an article, it is with regard to the participants that this is important.

This basic information is essential because, if sufficiently detailed, it gives important clues about the validity of the findings and the extent to which they can be generalized to others. If, for example, the participants were all Caucasian, an important question is whether the results can be generalized to those of a different ethnicity. This information is also critical in assisting you to determine whether appropriate statistical analyses were conducted (see Chapter 10). For example, if two groups differ significantly in age, and age is known to affect the main variable being measured in the study, then you will want to pay attention to whether the researchers controlled for age in their analyses (see Illustration 4.2).

In critiquing the Subjects/Participants section it is useful to ask the following questions:

- How were participants selected?
- How many participants dropped out of the study or did not respond?
- If there are multiple groups (or conditions), how were participants assigned to these?
- Were the groups homogeneous (i.e., uniform in their characteristics)?
- Is there evidence that the assignment method was reliable and valid?
- Are special circumstances, such as medication or treatment status of the participants, explained?

Illustration 4.2.   Does Age Influence Outcome?

Consider a study in which the researchers were interested in determining whether personality characteristics influenced pain severity ratings. Their hypothesis was that people who were outgoing and gregarious (i.e., extroverted), compared to those who were not (i.e., introverted), would have lower pain ratings in response to a painful situation. They selected two groups on the basis of a personality measure. One group included extroverts and the other group included introverts. The groups were similar in all other characteristics except age—the introverts were significantly older than the extroverts. In fact, most of the introverts were between 60 and 80 years whereas most of the extroverts were between 40 and 60 years. After exposing the participants to a pain-inducing procedure, they rated the severity of the pain they experienced on a scale anchored 0 = *no pain* to 10 = *very severe pain*. The researchers analyzed the data and found, as predicted, that the extroverts reported significantly less pain than the introverts. Thus, they concluded that extroverts experience less pain than introverts. But wait! What about age? Could the group differences in age influence the findings? This is a distinct possibility. Age might also influence (a) one's perception of pain, (b) the way pain-rating scales are interpreted, or (c) some other relevant aspect of whole experience. Thus, the findings might be the result of group differences in age rather than personality. Ideally, the researchers should have made sure the groups did not differ in age. Now that the data are collected, they might try to control, or account for, the group difference in age using a particular type of statistical analysis. Regardless, the lack of control for age in this study diminishes the degree of confidence that we can place in the researchers' conclusion that extroverts experience less pain than introverts.

Critiquing the Procedure Section.   The Procedure section also allows you to determine potential strengths and weaknesses of a study. Here there are many issues to consider. Indeed, depending on your familiarity with certain procedures, such as complex cognitive psychology paradigms or psychophysiological measurement techniques, some of these issues may be too advanced for you to critique easily. Nonetheless, there are a number of basic issues that can be considered regardless of the complexity of the study. You should always ask the following questions:

- Did the researcher unintentionally influence the participants in any way? In Chapter 8 we discuss this as an example of experimenter bias.

- Was the hypothesis or purpose of the study easy for the participants to figure out? Could this influence their performance or behavior? In Chapter 8 we discuss this as an example of participant bias.

- Were appropriate control groups used?

- Where appropriate, were double-blind procedures used? This type of procedure, discussed in Chapter 8, is important in studies where the effects of a treatment are being evaluated and refers to keeping *both* participants and researchers unaware of what treatment is being received by any given participant.

- If there was a manipulation, was a good rationale provided for the manipulation? Was any sort of manipulation check (to see if the manipulation worked) performed?

Critiquing the Design.   Critiquing the design gives an opportunity to evaluate the study's internal validity (or, the extent to which the study demonstrates that a variable of manipulation causes a change in the main variable being measured).

- If the researchers are trying to establish cause-effect, did they use an experimental design?

- Do the control groups adequately rule out alternative explanations?

- Did the researchers make the correct decision on the design they used, or would some other design have been more appropriate?

- Did the design fit the types of variables used (Chapter 9)?

Results

This section tells you, in statistical terms, what happened. It should begin with a brief description of the type of statistics that were used. Sometimes the description of statistical approach is provided in the Method section, and this is an entirely acceptable option. It is simply a matter of preference, with some researchers preferring to separate all description of what they have done from the actual results. In many cases, there is some presentation of the scores/measures that are being analyzed (again, unless this was done in the Method section). You must understand these before you can understand the results of the analyses. The authors should discuss briefly the results that relate specifically to their question or hypothesis. As well, other significant results may be mentioned. Once you have taken an advanced statistics course, the Results section may become easier to understand and evaluate. Nevertheless, *do not skip this section. It is the foundation on which the conclusions and related implications are based.* If you need assistance at this stage, we recommend that you try to get input from a mentor or colleague versed in statistics and, barring that, see if the information in Chapter 10 can be helpful.

When critiquing the Results section, the primary question to keep in mind is, "Are the statistical conclusions valid?" In addition to this general question, there are a number of specific questions that can be asked. These include the following:

- Were Type 1 errors (or, mistaking a chance difference for a real one) likely? The opposite of this is a Type 2 error, or, overlooking real difference and attributing it to chance.

- Were the right conditions being compared?

- Were statistical tests performed correctly? Were sufficient numbers of participants used to support the analysis? Did the authors ensure that assumptions of the test were not violated?

- Were appropriate follow-up tests done?

- If the authors report a null result, were Type 2 errors likely?

Discussion

This section should hold *no surprises*. That is, there should be very little, if any, new information presented here. The exception, of course, is that the researchers may buttress their description of the general or theoretical context in which the study and its results are to be interpreted. But, much of the foundation should have already been presented in the introductory remarks. It is also acceptable that the researchers speculate on the implications of their results and on potential directions for future research. And, a meticulously prepared article will usually identify limitations or shortcomings of the research.

If the authors get the results they expect, then the discussion should

- highlight main findings

- relate the findings to previous studies (which, for the most part, should have been mentioned in the Introduction)

- place the findings into a larger theoretical context

- list and discuss limitations of the study

- mention implications of the findings as they relate, for example, to clinical practice and future research directions

It is often the case that the results, or a portion of them, are contrary to expectation. In this case, the discussion will usually incorporate the aforementioned points along with a detailed explanation/reconciliation for the unexpected findings. Although there is sometimes a tendency to frown on negative or unexpected findings, these can, if adequately interpreted and explained, be as important as those that were expected. Negative or unexpected findings should never be simply dismissed.

Care needs to be taken when critiquing the Discussion. Remember that the authors are permitted to speculate in this section. However, sometimes authors state conclusions that are either contrary to the data or that go way beyond what the data would support. This is why we previously stated, and restate here, that it is of utmost importance to read the entire research article and not just the Introduction and Discussion. If you do not read the entire article, you may be accepting as accurate something that is not! Thus, it will be necessary for you to determine what is warranted on the basis of the presented results, what is acceptable and useful speculation, and what (if anything) seems to be unsupported.

Here are some useful questions to keep in mind when reviewing the discussion:

- Are the results accurately summarized?

- Are findings related to other research?

- Are the conclusions warranted, or do they go beyond the data?

- Are alternative explanations for the findings available? If so, are they explained?

- Are limitations of the study provided?

- Are clinical implications and future research directions outlined?

The critical questions outlined above are not meant to be complete. Rather, they represent the types of questions that can be asked when evaluating a research article. A table listing some of the specific questions that can be asked when critiquing a research article is provided in Illustration 4.3 (much of this is a summary of the material presented above). Keep this table handy when reading any research article and try to use it as a guide until the process becomes more or less automatic.

Step 3: Pulling It All Together

Now, armed with a summary of the critical points to look for in each section of a research article, let's turn our attention back to our model. When we introduce this model to our students, we have them role-play. What role do they play? That of a journal reviewer! This may be a "big step" for somebody just getting prepared to evaluate a research article critically, but, in our experience, it works well. So, when working through the steps outlined above, try thinking of yourself as somebody who has been asked by a journal editor to review and comment on a paper that has been submitted for publication. What are the responsibilities of reviewers that might aid you in your own critical reading? What are the characteristics of a well-prepared review?

The general responsibilities of a reviewer include the following:

- assess the quality and content of an article

- assess its strengths, weaknesses, and limitations (including all aspects from purpose through methods, analyses, and conclusions)

Illustration 4.3.   Critical Evaluation of Research Articles

---

1. Understand the message of the article.

2. Read the *entire* article.

3. Reread as necessary.

4. Consider the purpose of each section of the article and evaluate whether it meets the purpose.

5. Is the rationale for the study sound?

6. Are participants and selection procedures clearly described?

7. Is the research design well conceived and appropriate to the research question/hypothesis?

8. Are data and data analyses clearly and properly presented?

9. Are the data interpreted correctly and within their bounds?

10. Is there missing or superfluous information?

- provide comments on how it might be improved
- make a recommendation as to the suitability of an article for publication

In meeting these responsibilities, different reviewers usually focus on different aspects of an article. Indeed, each of us takes a slightly different approach. Journal editors, expecting this, often seek out reviewers who will emphasize different aspects of an article in their critiques. For example, some reviewers may attend more to the minute details of method and statistical analyses and others focus more on global and theoretical issues. Initially you might want to try to find a balance between these foci.

Regardless of focus, there are some characteristics of a review that journal editors find most useful. First, most begin with a summary or overview of the purpose, method, results, and conclusions of the study. Second, they provide details that focus on *relevant* weaknesses and shortcomings while minimizing concern about the minor flaws. As you read more research articles it will quickly become apparent that no study is perfect. The trick is deciding which flaws are of importance or "fatal" and which are not. Third, criticisms and recommendations for improvement are typically very specific and informative. Finally, the entire critique is presented in a supportive and constructive manner. This last point is very important, but unfortunately is one that is lost by a number of reviewers and can have detrimental effects on the entire process (Hadjistavropoulos & Bieling, 2000).

Illustration 4.4.   Samples of Reviewer Comments

Reviewer Feedback

Title: Generalized and nongeneralized performance anxiety and personality factors.

Author(s): Jane Doe and John Smith.

The general purpose of this study was to assess whether scores on measures of generalized and nongeneralized (i.e., circumscribed) performance anxiety are predicted by different aspects of personality. To address this issue, the authors administered a battery of questionnaires, including several measures of performance anxiety and personality factors, to an adequately large sample of university students. The authors provide a good rationale for choice of the scales used. Results obtained from stepwise multiple regression suggest that scores on the measure of circumscribed performance anxiety are predicted primarily by levels of state anxiety. On the other hand, the strongest predictor of generalized performance anxiety was trait neuroticism. The issue under investigation is of current relevance and provides new and important information to our current understanding and conceptualization of performance anxiety.

The article is, for the most part, well written, being sufficiently detailed yet concise. I do, however, have several points for the authors to consider. These are as follows:

1. In the Abstract, the authors note that the importance of their findings for assessing and conceptualizing performance anxiety are discussed in the article. I believe they have done a nice job of discussing conceptual issues. However, I am not sure that sufficient attention has been given to the implications of the study for assessment. I suggest that they flesh this out a bit. They may also wish to consider whether there are any treatment implications that can be offered on the basis of this data.

2. Because much of the research reviewed in the Introduction deals with clinical patients with severe performance anxiety, the authors need to strengthen their rationale for studying performance anxiety in university students. Though the issue is mentioned in the closing paragraph of the Discussion, more attention to the issue is warranted early in the article.

3. The authors mention that the correlations between their two measures of performance anxiety and trait neuroticism were significantly correlated; however, they have not provided the statistics to support this statement. Did the authors compare the differences between these correlations using appropriate statistical analyses? If so, this information should be reported. If not, the statement regarding significant differences should be omitted or restated. The addition of the proper statistics is perhaps the most appropriate solution.

(Continued)

Illustration 4.4. *(Continued)*

---

4. It would be beneficial to the reader to have some information about age (e.g., mean, standard deviation, range) of the participant sample. As well, observed ranges for the various measures used in the study (perhaps as an addition to the first table) would be beneficial. Readers not overly familiar with these measures would also benefit from an indication of the possible range of scores for each.

5. The first full paragraph on page 4 and the last paragraph beginning on page 10 are exceptionally long. This information would be clearer if the authors broke these paragraphs down into shorter units.

6. The authors make reference to several manuscripts submitted for publication that are dated by three years or more. Unless recently accepted for publication, it may be more appropriate to reference these manuscripts as unpublished data.

In Illustration 4.4 we provide a sample of a critique from a reviewer of a research article that was submitted for publication. This is an actual critique, but we have modified details so as to reduce the likelihood of your identifying the actual article that the review refers to. Our purpose in providing this example is to give you something tangible against which to compare and construct your own review summaries.

Summary

If you adopt our model of reviewing research articles, as outlined above, and carefully attend to the critical points of each section of a research article, then you are very likely to improve your critical evaluation skills. It may not be easy, and at times (particularly those times when entrenched in the Methods and Results sections) you may feel overwhelmed. If this is the case, seek help. And, persist. You will, thereby, get the most out of your reading efforts. We recommend that you practice this approach and, when possible, share and discuss your critiques of published studies with a mentor and colleagues. A journal club (i.e., a group of colleagues who get together on a regular basis to discuss one or more published articles) is an excellent forum for hearing others' critiques of research articles. It is also a place where you can compare your critiques against those of others and, in doing so, hone your skills.

It may take some time at first, but eventually you will become quite efficient at the process. In addition, because the processes of learning to read and to write about research are so intimately related, you will very likely notice substantial improvements in your ability to present your own research ideas effectively and concisely (see also Part 3 of this book). In fact, we are certain that applying the skills outlined in this chapter to your own research writing will assist you in creating a better piece of work.

References

Asmundson, G. J. G., & Taylor, S. (1996). Role of anxiety sensitivity in pain-related fear and avoidance. *Journal of Behavioral Medicine, 19,* 577–586.

Bellack, A. S., & Hersen, M. (Eds.). (1984). *Research methods in clinical psychology.* Elmsford, NY: Pergamon.

Campion, M. A. (1993). Editorial: Article review checklist: A criterion checklist for reviewing research articles in applied psychology. *Personnel Psychology, 46,* 705–718.

Epstein, S. (1995). What can be done to improve the journal review process. *American Psychologist, 50,* 883–885.

Eysenck, H. J., & Eysenck, S. B. (1992). Peer review: Advice to referees and contributors. *Personality and Individual Differences, 13,* 393–399.

Girden, E. R. (1996). *Evaluating research articles: From start to finish.* Thousand Oaks, CA: Sage.

Goldbeck-Wood, S. (1999). Evidence on peer review—Scientific quality control or smokescreen? *British Medical Journal, 318,* 44–45.

Hadjistavropoulos, T., & Bieling, P. J. (2000). When reviews attack: Ethics, free speech, and the peer review process. *Canadian Psychology, 41,* 152–159.

Kendall, P. C., Butcher, J. N., & Holmbeck, G. N. (Eds.). (1999). *Handbook of research methods in clinical psychology* (2nd ed.). New York: John Wiley.

Maher, B. A. (1978). A reader's, writer's, and reviewer's guide to assessing research reports in clinical psychology. *Journal of Consulting and Clinical Psychology, 46,* 835–838.

Oleson, K. C., & Arkin, R. M. (1996). Reviewing and evaluating a research article. In F. T. L. Leong & J. T. Austin (Eds.), *The psychology research handbook* (pp. 40–55). Thousand Oaks, CA: Sage.

Van Rooyen, S., Godlee, F., Evans, S., Black, N., & Smith, R. (1999). Effect of open peer review on quality of reviews and on reviewers' recommendations: A randomised trial. *British Medical Journal, 318,* 23–27.

5

Writing a Research Proposal

It is one thing to have a good research idea. It is another to put your idea on paper so that it can be conveyed to and understood (and, yes, criticized) by others. As we have noted in earlier chapters, research need not be a difficult and time-burdensome task. We would, however, be less than honest if we did not tell you that some research projects, or aspects of them, can be stressing and lengthy endeavors.

Indeed, although it may not be, the task of writing a research proposal can be a daunting one in some cases. It is often the most difficult part of the research venture, sometimes even more difficult than conducting the research itself. This is particularly the case when your research proposal is being submitted to a funding agency (Steinberg & Kennedy, 1995), where the competition for dollars is often fierce, or when preparing a thesis or dissertation. A well-written research proposal is not only a necessity in order to obtain funding and/or permission to begin your research, it is also a cornerstone of the entire research venture. A well-written research proposal provides the roadmap for the subsequent investigation. Therefore, in cases where a proposal is necessary, it is critical that it be crafted with the utmost care and precision.

In this chapter we cover the basics of writing a research proposal. Regardless of whether the proposal is being written for a thesis or dissertation or for consideration by a funding agency (i.e., a grant), certain elements are common, and the approach is similar. But there are some aspects where writing an academic research proposal is different from writing a grant application, and these are highlighted. If you are working under the supervision of a mentor, we recommend that each of these steps be reviewed and discussed with your mentor to ensure that you are on target.

Getting Started

So you've got a great research idea. Let's say you're interested in solving a puzzle that has mystified scholars for ages—the question of why some people like smooth peanut butter and others prefer chunky. (This is just an example. If you were actually thinking about this particular question, we strongly suggest that you go back and read Chapter 4, "Is the Idea Worth Researching?") Let's presume you have a specific hypothesis—People who prefer chunky are more likely to be extroverted than those who prefer smooth. You have based this hypothesis on a voluminous published literature, most of it in the highly cited *International Journal of Arachidology*. Although others have alluded to this hypothesis, you conclude that no one has heretofore had the intestinal fortitude and the burning curiosity to resolve this issue definitively. Of course, the other possibilities are (a) it was an inane idea, so no one tackled it; (b) it was a trivial problem, so no one cared; or (c) others have tried and failed and were unable to publish their results. Expect to spend considerable time writing your research proposal. A good thesis or dissertation proposal will probably take several months of preparation, including anywhere from 20 to 50 hours of actually sitting at the computer, writing. So you need to plan ahead, give yourself ample time to do the writing, get feedback from others, make changes, and then complete the final draft. Inevitably, you will find yourself fighting deadlines, and this can be stressful. Do yourself a favor and get started early. Begin by mapping out a time line for how and when you will complete the various phases of your writing.

Let's say your dissertation proposal is due in 6 months. Start now by putting your hypothesis in writing. Conduct your online literature search. Sit in the library and pull the articles from the *International Journal of Arachidology* that relate to your topic, and retrieve the additional references that you'll uncover while reading these seminal papers. This will enable you to get a good feel for what is known about the topic you are investigating. Find out who the "big names" in the field are and be sure to read some of their earlier work. You may find that Professor Donald Kraft, prior to devoting his life's work to the study of peanut butter-related behavior, spent 10 years studying the appetitive escapades of the Northern Alaskan smelt. It turns out that smelts have an incredible affinity for peanut butter, causing them to become trapped in sandwiches discarded by careless fishermen. And, many of the fishermen who throw their sandwiches overboard are raving extroverts. Knowing this lets you make this connection in your proposal, thereby demonstrating your impressive command of the background literature, if not your capacity to separate the wheat from the chaff.

Make certain that you are investing your effort in a topic that is significant, not already investigated to death, and—of utmost importance—of interest to you. You will be investing plenty of sweat equity into your written proposal, so be sure that the topic excites you sufficiently that you're willing to invest that effort.

Know the Format

What format is your research proposal supposed to follow? Every institution and granting agency has somewhat different requirements for the written document. Early in the process get this information in writing so you can refer to it repeatedly. Here are some of the things you will need to know about the format.

Relevant Sections

What are the various sections that are required in the written document? These are highlighted in Illustration 5.1. Typically, sections that are to be included are

- Introduction (this usually includes a statement about the rationale and importance of the topic to be studied)

- Background (a succinct review of the relevant literature—and we emphasize the word *relevant*)

- Specific Aims and Hypotheses

- Research Design and Methods (often with subsections)

- Progress Report or Preliminary Data (for most grant applications)

- References

- Budget

- Appendix (included here might be copies of some of your previous relevant publications; letters of support from collaborators; letters of agreement from outside agencies. Check the instructions to see what is and what is not permitted here. The Appendix is *not* the place to put things that didn't fit in the body of the proposal because you exceeded the page limit.)

Although some latitude is often provided in the case of thesis or dissertation proposals, granting organizations tend to be merciless in their insistence that applicants adhere to the prescribed formats. This is mandatory for granting agencies because they must ensure that every applicant plays by the same rules. You may write a marvelously lucid and insightful grant application, but if you put it in the wrong format, you could be out of luck. Even if the agency doesn't return your grant outright, consider that

Illustration 5.1.   Anatomy of a Research Proposal

Introduction
The Introduction most often includes a statement about the rationale and importance of the topic to be studied.

Background
The Background provides a succinct review or overview of the literature that is specific to the topic being studied.

Specific Aims/Hypotheses
This section provides a clear, concise listing of the study aims, hypotheses, or both. It must be very brief.

Research Methods
The Research Methods gives the precise details about what you propose to do. Its organization can vary but typically includes subsections on design particulars and time lines, description of participants, the precise methodological approach, and a power calculation (although this might be placed in a separate section).

Progress Report
This section is used to highlight your findings from related research applicable to the topic being studied.

References
The reference section provides citations to all papers, reviews, published tests, and book chapters mentioned in the sections listed above.

Budget
This section states the amount of financial request and provides a detailed justification for it. It is not applicable to theses, dissertations, and some small grants.

Appendix
The Appendix includes materials such as previous publications relevant to the proposal, elaborations of information or flow charts that clarify the study protocol, and technical materials. It is not a place to include more of what should have been fit within the application's body proper.

reviewers may reasonably ask the question, "If the applicant can't read the instructions on how to complete the application, how likely is it that he or she is capable of doing the research?"

Length Requirements and Limitations

How long should the proposal be? There are always page limitations for research proposals. Very often there are also restrictions on the length of various sections (e.g., Methods). Know the rules and abide by them. Don't try to skirt the rules by using a tiny font to fit more information into the same space. First, most proposals specify the minimum font size (usually either 10 or 12 points). Second, although you may achieve your goal of putting more words on the same number of pages, you will also run the risk of annoying the people who need to read the proposal and wind up with a headache from squinting at your indecipherable document. Not a good idea.

Additional Materials

What additional components are required? Forms, forms, forms. These are the bane of any researcher's existence. Thesis and dissertation proposals don't often need a lot beyond the names and signatures of the responsible student and adviser(s). But grant applications usually require a plethora of documentation that is ancillary to the research proposal itself. These include things like face pages with names and contact information for the institutional representatives responsible for the grant (e.g., departmental grants manager), along with names and signatures of the designated institutional authorities (e.g., department chair; dean). Also usually required is written evidence of human participants' approval, sometimes including a copy of the actual approved informed consent document. Don't wait until the last minute to collect these additional documents.

Preparing an Introduction

The Introduction is the part of the proposal that succinctly states what you are going to do, why you are going to do it, and what you expect to find. Like any good beginning, it should capture the readers' (in this case, either your thesis/dissertation committee members' or the grant reviewers') attention and make them want to read more. This is usually best accomplished by quickly getting to the heart of the matter—Why is this an important topic to research? What will be learned from this effort? How will it advance our knowledge?

Not every research topic needs to be earth shattering. In fact, as we have discussed in earlier chapters, most research advances the field in small, sometimes tiny, increments. So, the goal is not to inflate the value of your research project to make it sound like the next step on the way to the cure for cancer. (If it is the next step on the way to the cure for cancer, you'll probably need to say very little—the research will speak for itself.) The goal is merely to help the reader understand the merits of your project, and to do so in a way that emphasizes how the work you propose fits in with what has already been done and what remains to be done in the near future.

In the case of the Peanut Butter Hypothesis, you would want to point out that personal preferences for comestibles are of considerable interest to agricultural producers and food manufacturers alike. You would want to note that peanuts are of special interest because of their many uses, including peanut oil, peanut sauce, peanut skin cream (try it), and the most infamous of all—peanut butter. Peanut butter is beloved by children throughout North America, but parents are faced with the daunting task of trying to remember which of their children likes smooth and which likes crunchy. Mixing them up could lead to a sandwich being thrown in the trash, or even worse, traded for tuna salad. If it could be proven that certain personality types liked certain peanut butter types, the information could be used to help parents develop mnemonics for remembering which child liked which (e.g., Peter is the *T*alkative one, he likes smoo*T*h).

Preparing the Background

The Background is the part of the application where you demonstrate your awareness of prior research on the topic and where you place your own project in context. It should be based on a thorough review of the literature, usually best conducted with an online search supplemented by the pulling of references that appear in the papers you read. Dissertation proposals are generally expected to be exhaustively thorough, whereas you have more latitude in a grant application to cite the literature that is most directly relevant to your proposal. In fact, in the case of grant applications, the page limitations necessitate that you discuss only the most germane literature. There simply isn't room to cover it all.

This section of the proposal should not regurgitate, or even merely summarize, the relevant literature. It should be your synthesis of the literature. It should contain *your interpretation* of the findings and *your critique* of this prior work. People reading this section of the proposal don't just want to know what has been done before. They want to know what *you* think of it, and why.

A good Background section will provide a strong set-up for the Specific Aims and Hypotheses section. Having read your interpretation of the studies that have come before, the reader should find him- or herself thinking about what needs to be done next—presumably precisely the things you'll be proposing in the next section.

Preparing the Specific Aims and/or Hypotheses

You usually have the option of delineating the goals of your project either as Specific Aims (i.e., what you will do; sometimes also referred to as

"Objectives") or as Hypotheses (i.e., what you expect to find). In some cases, it is worthwhile spelling things out in both formats. Some projects will have only one aim and one corresponding hypothesis, whereas some others will have several. Rarely should a proposal contain more than three or four specific aims and corresponding hypotheses. If you find yourself writing a proposal that is asking more than three or four distinct questions, then consider narrowing your scope of inquiry to just one or two. Remember, you need to keep things manageable and feasible.

This section of the proposal should be extremely brief, rarely more than a page in total. It is often best presented in point form, to whit:

- Specific Aim 1: To determine whether particular personality characteristics are associated with peanut butter consistency preferences.

- Hypothesis 1: Extroverts will prefer chunky peanut butter.

Preparing the Methods Section

This is the section of the proposal that details precisely what you will do. It should be organized in a way that makes sense for the kind of research you are conducting. You may wish to begin with a brief Overview, a paragraph or two broadly outlining the study design (e.g., "I will conduct a survey of peanut butter type preferences in a community sample of men and women living in Rutabaga County . . ."). This is a good place to indicate the duration of your study and the timeline for its conduct. For example, "The survey will begin in the first quarter of next year and will take 6 months to complete. Data entry and analysis will require an additional 6 months. The proposed duration of the study in its entirety is thus 12 months."

Participants

For research that involves human participants, next comes a description of who those participants will be and how they will be selected. For example, "Participants will be a randomly selected sample of 1,200 men and women age 18 to 65 living in Rutabaga County. Participants over the age of 65 will be excluded, as will younger participants with dentures, given that previous research has demonstrated a profound dislike for peanut butter in these groups that transcends individual differences. Furthermore, participants who report being allergic to peanut butter will be excluded for obvious reasons." It is often useful (and sometimes required) to provide a breakdown, based on your previous knowledge of residents of Rutabaga County (e.g., from the most recent census), what proportion of men and women and from what age and ethnic groups you expect to sample. For example, "Based on population estimates from the most recent U.S. census, conducted in 2000, we expect our sample to consist of approximately equal numbers of men and women; 30% of participants will be between the ages of 18 and 35, 40% will be between the ages of 36 and 50, and 30% will be between the ages of 51 and 65; ethnic breakdown is expected to be approximately 20% Black, 50% Caucasian, 20% Hispanic, and 10% Other."

Methods

This is the part where you describe, in considerable detail, what you will do with the participants. You may choose to break it down into subsections that are appropriate for your study. For example, we might have subheadings for our study such as "Survey Design and Sampling Methods," "Selection and Training of Interviewers," "Questionnaire and Other Measures," and "Payment of Participants." Be as detailed as possible— within the page limits—about your methods. Adequately describe the characteristics of the instruments you will use—How precise are they? How reliable are they? Cite the literature to support your claims in this regard. The Methods section should also explain to the reader *why* you made the particular methodological decisions you did. For example, if you were aware of a dozen different questionnaires to measure personality, why did you choose the Carter Personality Questionnaire? You want to demonstrate to the reviewers that you were aware of other options, and that your decisions were thoughtfully made.

Power Analysis and Statistical Analysis

It is beyond the scope of this chapter to present a detailed treatise on statistics. Rather, we merely want to point out the fact that you will need to pay considerable attention to the statistical methods you will use in your study, and that you will need to document them here. Specifically, you will need to include details of your power analysis and your planned statistical analyses.

Every research proposal should include a power analysis that shows how many participants are required to test the study's main hypothesis without falling prey to Type II error (i.e., falsely accepting the null hypothesis). If you have pilot data to guide your power analysis, use them. But often you will have no pilot data, meaning that you must rely on other published studies to obtain the needed estimates for the power analysis. At other times, in the complete absence of published studies using your outcome measures, you must resort to using effect sizes, of which there are several indexes (Cohen, 1992) the simplest of which is the zero order correlation, to inform your power analysis. Although this is really a shot in the dark, and will be recognized as such by reviewers of your proposal, it is better than nothing. In this day and age it is just not acceptable to start a study without a vague idea of how many participants will be required. Cohen (1992) provides a good primer on power analysis.

The power analysis must mesh well with the Participants section of your proposal. If your power analysis indicates that you will need 300 participants to test your Peanut Butter Hypothesis, then you want to be sure that you have specified that you will include at least 300 participants in the study. And you will have wanted to demonstrate that this number is feasible. If, realistically, you will be able to recruit only 40 participants during the course of your study, then there's no point doing the study—and your proposal would (or at least should) not be approved. You would either need to think of a way to include more participants, switch to measures that will have more robust effects, or go back to the drawing board and come up with a new study.

Separate from the power analysis is the section on Statistical Analysis. This is often approached as an afterthought, but is a very important section of your proposal and should not get short shrift. This is the part of your proposal that shows the reviewers that (a) you actually know what you're going to do with the mounds of data you plan on collecting, and (b) you're really going to use the data to test the hypotheses you pose. We often write this part of the proposal to match up directly with each of the hypotheses. For example, we'd say, "Logistic regression analysis will be used to test the hypothesis that extroverts prefer crunchy peanut butter. Scores on the extroversion measure will be used to predict membership in either the crunchy or smooth groups. Given the extant literature showing that gender may influence peanut butter type preferences, these analyses will be run separately for men and women." Remember, be specific here. The reviewer, whether your supervisor or grant referee, will use your description to scrutinize the extent to which you know what you are doing.

Preparing the Literature References

Check to see if there are limits on the number of citations you can include, then whittle them down to leave just the references that are most important to your proposal. It isn't necessary to cite every paper ever written on the subject. It is necessary, though, to include the most recent papers (an out-of-date set of references is a turn-off for most reviewers), the seminal papers, and papers containing controversial findings. Never try to conceal—by not citing—papers that don't fit with your hypothesis. Rather, acknowledge the divergent results and discuss how your proposed study will help bring clarity to this area of research.

Preparing a Budget

Budgets are not usually required for dissertation proposals (although they probably should be, if only as a good learning opportunity for the future), but are *almost* always required for grant applications. Some grant types have dollar limits, so be sure that you can accomplish the research you propose within these limits.

There are some smaller, private foundation grants that do not require highly detailed budgets. They are the exception. Here we consider what might be necessary in a situation where a high degree of detail is required. In this case, the goal of the budget is to provide the funding agency with a realistic assessment of how much money you need to get the study done. You want to show the reviewers that you are cognizant of the demands of your proposal and that you have an organized approach to seeing that the demands are met. You want to *justify* everything (or almost everything) you request. This means that you will describe what the person (or piece of equipment) will do, how it fits into the project needs, and what it will cost. If you ask for a more expensive piece of equipment when cheaper alternatives are available, then you want to justify why you need the more expensive version (e.g., it does something special that the others do not, and this is necessary for the project because ...).

Breaking the project(s) down into tasks, and then determining who will perform which tasks over what time frame, is a useful approach to budget planning. You translate these estimates into personnel and materials required per funding period.

For example, the Peanut Butter Study requires that the following tasks be performed:

1. Examine census data and prepare telephone randomization list

2. Telephone participants to describe the nature of the study and inquire about their interest in participating

3. Mail questionnaires and consent forms to 1,200 willing participants

4. Track rates of refusal and questionnaire return, and mail reminders

5. Collate returned questionnaires and enter data into computerized database

6. Re-enter the data to check for errors

7. Do the statistical analysis

8. Prepare the Abstract for meeting and manuscript for submission to peer-reviewed journal

You have already decided that you want to complete the surveying of 1,200 respondents in 6 months. To meet this goal, you know (based on prior experience—your own or that of your advisor or collaborators) that you will need to employ four half-time (20 hours per week) research assistants for 4 months, after which you can drop down to two half-time research assistants (also 20 hours per week) for 2 months to finish off contacting the stragglers. In the second 6 months, two part-time research assistants (each 10 hours per week) can handle the data entry and check the requirements.

You may also decide to employ a statistical consultant for 20 hours per week to provide advice about the data analysis. Although it behooves everyone who does research to be well informed about statistics, it is not expected that you do it all yourself. It is becoming increasingly common to rely on a statistical expert to advise about how to analyze the data, and, in some cases, to do it (or supervise someone else who will do it). In fact, unless you are an accomplished statistician yourself, the absence of a statistician on a grant application can be seen as a glaring omission. Finding (and hiring) a statistical consultant will take some advance thinking and networking. Find out from colleagues whom they have worked with in the past and see if that person is available. If not, ask that person if he or she can recommend a statistical consultant who might be available and interested. At some institutions, statistical consultants are available as a "resource." That is, the institution hires them and you can request or buy (from your grant) a piece of their time.

Once you have identified the requisite personnel, you would describe and justify them in the application and put a dollar figure on the total. There will typically be someone at your institution (in the Office of Grants Management or in Sponsored Programs) who will give you the salary and benefit amounts for the type of personnel you need.

In addition to personnel, what else will you need to do in the study? Will you need to rent additional telephone lines for the surveyors? What will it cost to duplicate (or purchase, if they are copyrighted) the questionnaires? What will postage cost? Will you be paying participants an honorarium to participate? These materials or supplies should be detailed and justified.

Some funding agencies permit requests for funds for travel to professional meetings. To the extent that you will be presenting findings from your project and/or interacting with other researchers whose work relates to your own, this is a justifiable and worthwhile expense.

Preparing an Appendix

Some applications allow you to provide additional information or materials in an Appendix. What can go in the Appendix? This depends on the instructions that go along with the specific type of proposals. Often this is the place to include previous publications (your own, those of your collaborators, or sometimes even critical articles from other authors that you refer to in your paper). Sometimes you are permitted to include more elaborate information about the study protocol than you can fit into the body of the grant: things like a detailed therapist manual for a particular type of psychotherapy, or a description of methods for the new bio-assay you will be conducting as part of the research. Photographs or other technical materials may also be included here.

The Appendix is not the place to include more of what should have been confined to the required page limit of the body of the grant itself. Trying to do so will only annoy the reviewers and, even worse, may result in the application being returned to you by the agency.

After You've Written It . . .

Get other opinions from peers and supervisors. Even an outside read from someone relatively unfamiliar with the subject matter can be extremely helpful. First, they may pick up typographical and grammatical errors that you, being so close to the material, have overlooked. They can also be helpful with the content. Remember that the grant reviewer(s), although probably conversant with the topic, will not necessarily be extremely familiar with your area of research. It is, therefore, important not to write for the super-expert, but rather to aim your writing at an intelligent generalist in your field. Having someone outside your own research cadre read the application can help ensure that this criterion is met.

Summary

Writing a research proposal is the penultimate expression of your research ideas and questions. It is when you put your hypotheses on the line, make predictions about what you expect to find, and document how you will get the answers. A research proposal should be succinct, thereby demonstrating your capacity to think efficiently and in a highly goal-directed manner. It is your chance not just to show the reader what you think, but *how* you think. A research proposal should be constructed with considerable thought and advance planning; this takes much time and cannot be left to the last minute. Read the instructions for the application carefully and be certain that you follow the prescribed guidelines. Write for the intelligent generalist, not for the expert: explain (or, better yet, limit the use of) uncommon terms, and lay out for the reader the reasons that this study should be performed and how it will advance the field. When you're happy with your interim written product, get a colleague to read and critique it. Then take the suggestions to heart and revise your proposal accordingly. A well-written research proposal will not only let you achieve your goal of getting permission and/or funding to carry out the study—it will also serve as a roadmap for actually doing the work later on. For this reason, whether or not your goal is funding, every study you plan should, time permitting for those inundated with clinical duties, begin with a research proposal.

References

Cohen, J. (1992). A power primer. *Psychological Bulletin, 112,* 155–159.
Steinberg, J., & Kennedy, C. (1995). Successful research grant application. In H. A. Pincus (Ed.), *Research funding and resource manual* (pp. 21–38). Washington, DC: American Psychiatric Association.

6

A Primer on Research Ethics

L et's assume you now have a good idea and you have decided to invest time in systematically evaluating it. When you set out to write your research proposal, a necessary component, as described in Chapter 5, is the detailed description of the methods to be employed. The method, or your approach to collecting the data you need to meet your objectives, is necessarily closely linked to your idea. The method is also closely linked to another issue—research ethics. Is your study ethical? Are participants taking part voluntarily? Do aspects of your method put them at risk and, if so, in what way? Do participants understand this? Are other aspects of the method understood?

These are the types of questions that need to be considered carefully during the planning of your research. They should not be considered as afterthoughts but, rather, as an integral and ongoing part of the research process. They are also the types of questions that will be asked by your Research Ethics Board or Institutional Review Board (hereafter referred to collectively as IRB). Most, if not all, universities and hospitals have IRBs charged with ensuring that ethical considerations are not overlooked. The IRB will carefully scrutinize your answers to these questions during their deliberations about your proposed research plan.

General Principles

The purpose of this chapter is to provide some general principles and guidelines that will assist you in ensuring that your research plans are ethical. It is not meant to provide a comprehensive coverage of ethical issues as they relate to clinical research. These can be gleaned from the ever-developing literature on the topic (e.g., Bersoff & Bersoff, 1999; Hyman, 1999; Michels, 1999; Roberts & Roberts, 1999).

It is also beyond our scope to consider various professional codes of ethics that have been written to address ethical concerns related to both clinical practice and research. There are many, and we recommend that you become well acquainted with them. The following general principles transcend disciplines and, therefore, warrant mentioning here.

1. The welfare, integrity, and rights of potential participants in a research project must take precedence over everything else.

2. The welfare, integrity, and rights of potential participants in a research project must not be violated.

3. Potential participants have the right to be informed about the nature and purpose of any research project that they are considering taking part in.

4. Potential participants have the right to be informed about the potential benefits and, perhaps more important, the potential risks of participating. And, if the study involves an intervention or treatment, they have the right to be informed about alternative treatment approaches over and above that used in the study.

5. Potential participants have the right to refuse participation without being penalized for doing so. Likewise, participants have the right to withdraw from a study at any time after entering it, without being penalized for doing so.

6. Participants have the right to have any information derived from their participation kept confidential.

From the perspective of the researcher, these general principles may sound restrictive and potentially constraining. To some, they may even seem adversarial to the objectives of research. It is not surprising, then, that an IRB enforcing these principles is often viewed as the evil and foreboding nemesis of the researcher. But, for the sake of participants, they are *absolutely* necessary. Without them, it can be difficult for researchers to find a balance between the responsibility of maintaining the rights of their participants and the desire (and need) to advance knowledge and understanding in their particular area of interest. An example may be useful here.

Between 1932 and 1972 the U.S. Public Health Service conducted an observational evaluation, commonly known as the Tuskegee Study, of more than 400 Black male sharecroppers with untreated syphilis. The purpose of this study was to document the natural course of syphilis and racial differences in its clinical manifestations. The men were *not* told that they had syphilis. And, because they were not told they had the disease, they were also not told how to prevent spreading it, and they were not given any treatment. Indeed, they were not given treatment even though an effective cure for syphilis was discovered during the course of the study.

This study is notorious for its lack of regard for participants. It is still widely commented on in the literature (see recent review by White, 2000) and still receives airtime on television documentaries. Among other things (e.g., instructing on exploitation of vulnerable populations for research purposes), the study serves to underscore the importance of balancing rights of participants with advancing clinical knowledge. In this case, there was no balance. The welfare and integrity of participants were apparently ignored. Most participant rights were violated. Indeed, participants were not informed of the nature and purpose of the study, they were not informed about potential risks (to themselves or others), they were not allowed to refuse participation or withdraw, and, related to this last point, they were not offered medication once it became available. Clearly, the costs (to participants) of obtaining knowledge of the natural course of syphilis outweighed the medical science and societal value added by that knowledge, particularly when a cure was available.

A Model for Making Ethical Decisions

It seems a given that any research project should (or must) balance the rights of potential participants with the desire to better understand some aspect of a condition. Most of us are not bad people with a predisposition to act in an unethical or immoral manner. Rather, ethical problems in research most often arise as a result of good, conscientious people making poor decisions about certain aspects of their research purposes or methods.

So, how do we make good, ethical decisions about our research? This is a question with no easy answer. We, like Bersoff and Bersoff (1999), are of the opinion that a good knowledge of ethical principles combined with a firm grasp of research methods and a touch of creativity will allow a researcher to "find a way to research an issue in an ethical manner" (p. 34). Below we present a stepwise approach, modeled on the Canadian Code of Ethics for Psychologists (Canadian Psychological Association, 1991), that we have found useful for putting these words into practice. More detailed approaches not specific to research, but applicable to it, have been presented by other authors (e.g., Bersoff & Bersoff, 1999; Hadjistavropoulos & Malloy, 2000; Koocher & Keith-Spiegel, 1998).

Identify Potential Areas Where the Rights of Participants May Be Violated.
Ethical issues in research are often closely tied to aspects of the method you
are using. So, a firm understanding of methodological issues and options
can aid greatly in making ethical decisions. We recommend that less experienced researchers partake in an in-depth discussion about methodology with
an adviser or mentor. The decisions made by an inexperienced researcher
can be informed by such discussions with colleagues.

**Identify and Consider Alternative Methods That You Can Use in Conducting
Your Study.** There are often many methods that can be used to answer the
same question. Different methods impact on the rights of participants to
different degrees. Some methods involve more risks (short-term, long-term,
or both) than do others. For example, in an attempt to learn more about
road rage, it would be more risky to incite and observe the rage in a natural
setting than to simulate it in the laboratory or to interview people about it.
Alternatives also need to be weighed against each other in terms of time to
participate, demands of participation, necessary resources, overall costs,
expected time lines, and so on.

Choose a Course of Action. What is the best alternative among those
identified? All other things being equal, use of a less-risky method would
constitute the more ethical decision. In many cases, though, it is not the
least risky method that is going to advance knowledge. Your decision needs
to balance these two issues.

**Implement Your Decided Course of Action, Monitor Its Consequences, and
Assume Responsibility for It.** This is the step where your decision is put into
action. Presumably, it is a decision that, based on your current understanding of all relevant information, balances participant rights with your efforts
to derive new and important knowledge. In monitoring your decision, you
will continuously evaluate the consequences of your choice. If anything
changes such that participants rights are jeopardized (e.g., you learn that
the treatment you are testing has serious adverse effects, a new and effective treatment becomes available for the condition you are evaluating), you
will need to re-engage in the decision-making process.

Each research project will have its own unique set of ethical considerations. Attention to each of the aforementioned points should help ensure
that you are approaching all aspects of your research in an ethical manner.
Your IRB will, of course, also assist you in this respect. If your institution
or place of employment does not have an IRB, then we recommend that you

seek one out (through a local hospital or university) and request that their IRB comment on the project for you.

Each IRB will have its own specific expectations, some mandated and others not. Similar to our recommendations with regard to research proposals and grants, it is good practice to acquaint yourself with the submission requirements (likely forms, forms, and more forms) and deadlines of your IRB. In most cases (we discuss possible exceptions below) you will be required to present potential participants with an information sheet and consent form (which are sometimes combined into a single form). These are primary tools by which you, as the researcher, and your IRB, as a representative of your organization and societal interests, can ensure balance between participant rights and advancing knowledge.

Informed Consent

Perhaps the most effective means of ensuring that the welfare and rights of research participants (or potential participants) are not violated is to inform them, in general terms, about the research purposes and method, and then allow them to decide if they wish to participate. This process is referred to as *informed consent*. Information is generally presented in a written format but can be accompanied by a verbal delivery. In fact, as potential participants often fail to read information presented to them (Mann, 1994), the verbal accompaniment is a good idea—it gives you greater certainty that the information is actually received and understood. If, based on this information, a person decides to participate in your study, then you can enroll him or her and start collecting data. But, if he or she declines, then data should not (or, ethically, can't) be collected.

Notice that we suggest that informed consent is based on the provision of *general information*. What do we mean by this? Well, several things.

First, the information needs to be written in language that is easily understood by potential participants. It should be clear and concise, without complex and technical terminology or jargon.

Second, it should summarize the study purpose, pertinent aspects of the method (particularly, what the participants will do and how long it will take them), and participant rights. It need not necessarily reveal the specific question or hypothesis that is being evaluated. There are, indeed, many instances (particularly in some areas of psychological research) where revealing this information would influence the participants' responses or behaviors and, thus, compromise validity of the data. In some cases, withholding information or initially deceiving participants is acceptable—the Tuskegee Study not being one of them—and legal.

For example, participants might be told that they are being asked to partake in a study comparing an active medication to a placebo. The chances of receiving the active medication are one in two. In this type of study, knowing whether one is receiving placebo or active medication may influence response (by the participant, the therapist, or both). Thus, this information is withheld from both the participant and the therapist (until the end of the study, or if the patient drops out due to side effects) so that observed effects, if any, can be attributed to the active medication and not to expectancies.

Where possible, withholding information from participants should be kept to a minimum. Deception should be avoided if alternate methodological approaches to addressing the same idea are available (for a more detailed discussion of informed consent and deception, see Bersoff & Bersoff, 1999).

Informed Consent in Special Populations

The concept of informed consent assumes that information is received, understood, and, on that basis, a decision of whether or not to participate is made. There are, however, some groups where special considerations are necessary, as they may not be considered legally competent to provide informed consent. When participants are children, for example, informed consent must be obtained from parents or legal guardians. Nevertheless, children *must* be provided with a sufficient description of the study and be asked to assent verbally to participating. The description given to children should be given in a way that facilitates their ability to understand their rights as participants. Should a child wish not to participate in a study, his or her choice must preempt parental consent.

Adults with cognitive impairment (e.g., dementia, closed head injury), as well as those with severe mental illness (e.g., schizophrenia), should *not* be assumed to be unable to give informed consent to participate in a study. In these cases, we recommend that you assess the ability of each potential participant to understand his or her rights and the implications of providing consent. On the other hand, a legally incompetent person is, by definition, not autonomous and can't give a legally or ethically valid consent. In such cases, informed consent can be sought from the person's legal guardian.

Exceptions to Informed Consent

There are some instances in which your IRB may not require a *signed* consent form. Again, because of considerable variability, you need to check whether these exceptions are applicable to you. Research involving mass screening with self-report questionnaires may not require written informed consent provided that details of the study are given via a cover letter. Voluntary completion of the self-report questionnaires is often regarded as acceptable consent. Surveys administered by telephone often do not require a signed consent form. In part, this is a concession to the near impossibility of obtaining written consent over the telephone, balanced with the ease with which participants can choose not to participate (i.e., they say "No thank you" or just hang up). Nonetheless, the IRB typically reviews all materials, including the introductory and explanatory statements as well as the questions themselves, in advance. Likewise, requirements of informed consent may be waived when information is being gleaned from patient records or some other forms of archived data (hair or nail clippings being less controversial than samples of genetic material). As a rule, if you are uncertain about whether an exemption to informed consent applies to your study, check with your IRB.

Parts of the Information and Consent Form

Here we present the essential parts of the information sheet and consent form (which, hereafter, we refer to as the Information and Consent Form). Examples of the type of information to include are also provided, as is a sample copy of an Information and Consent Form (see Illustration 6.1).

Introduction. In your introductory information you should identify yourself, explain the general purpose of your study, describe the procedure (i.e., what the participant will be asked to do), and give an estimate of the time that will be required to participate. As we suggest above, it is a good idea to keep this information general in nature. It does, however, need to be of sufficient detail that it serves to inform.

Benefits and Risks/Discomforts. You may wish to present information about potential benefits as well as risks and discomforts together. Or, you can present these as separate sections of your Information and Consent Form. We prefer the latter approach in more complex studies.

When describing potential benefits you should indicate that new information will be derived that may be of considerable scientific and practical value. If this were not the case, then you would not likely be conducting the study. You should also indicate whether the participants will benefit directly from their participation. For example, will participation help

(Text continued on page 74)

Illustration 6.1.   Sample Information and Consent Form

Dr. Gordon J. G. Asmundson and Dr. Heather D. Hadjistavropoulos
Clinical Research and Development

SELECTIVE ATTENTION IN DEPRESSION AND PANIC DISORDER
INFORMATION FOR POTENTIAL PARTICIPANTS

INVITATION TO PARTICIPATE: We are inviting you to participate in this investigation if you have been experiencing current episodes of major depression or panic attacks. We are also extending this invitation to you if you have never experienced either of these conditions. The investigation is being conducted by Drs. Gordon Asmundson and Heather Hadjistavropoulos at the Clinical Research and Development Program of the Regina Health District.

PURPOSE OF THE INVESTIGATION: Previous research has indicated that people with severe depression and/or anxiety develop specific ways of thinking and attending to their environment in order to help them cope with their condition. The research, however, has provided inconsistent results as to whether individuals with depression differ from those with anxiety in the way they attend to things in their environment. Understanding these conditions and how they differ from each other is important if we are to improve the effectiveness of available treatments.

PROCEDURE: If you decide to participate in this investigation, two appointments will be scheduled for you at the Clinical Research and Development Program. These appointments will be at least two days apart. You may eat a meal before coming to your appointments but we request that you do not have any caffeine (such as coffee, tea, cola, or chocolate) or alcohol before you arrive. We also request that you wear your contact lenses or bring your reading glasses if you use these. Upon your arrival for each appointment, you will be asked to complete four brief questionnaires that ask about your experiences with symptoms of depression and anxiety over the past week. Thereafter, you will complete several computerized tasks. No special computer skills or familiarity with computers is needed to complete these tasks. The computer task on the first appointment will involve reading aloud the top word of a word pair presented on a computer monitor and then, after some word pair presentations, pressing the space bar on the computer keyboard as quickly as possible when you see a small dot appear on the screen. The computer task on the second appointment will involve naming aloud and as quickly as possible the color that words are presented in while attempting to ignore the meaning of the words. You will do the computer tasks by yourself in a private room. An investigator will be in an adjacent room and you will be able to talk to him or her by an intercom if you have questions or need assistance. Each appointment will take about 60 minutes.

(Continued)

Illustration 6.1. *(Continued)*

POTENTIAL BENEFITS: The results of this investigation may produce information that will be of considerable benefit to the scientific community and, ultimately, to people who are receiving treatment for major depression and/or panic disorder. There may not be any direct benefit to you that results from participating. However, if some important information regarding your condition becomes known as a result of your participation we will, with your written permission, share it with your treatment provider.

POTENTIAL RISKS AND DISCOMFORTS: There are no known risks or discomforts associated with participation in this investigation. The only cost to you will be the time needed to attend the appointments and complete the questionnaires and tasks (about 2 hours in total). We will make every effort to schedule appointments at a time that is most convenient for you. We will also provide you with a $30 honorarium to help pay for your travel and other expenses that may result from your participation.

CONFIDENTIALITY: Any information gained from your participation in this investigation is confidential and will be shared only with members of the research team involved in the investigation. Information will be used for research purposes and any details that may reveal your identity will be excluded from research reports and presentations. As noted above, if some important information regarding your condition becomes known as a result of your participation we will, with your written permission, share it with your treatment provider.

VOLUNTARY PARTICIPATION: Your participation in this investigation is entirely voluntary. Should you choose not to participate, or if you wish to withdraw from the investigation at any time after starting, you may do so without any consequences to your current or future treatment.

OFFER TO ANSWER QUESTIONS: Please feel free to ask any questions that you may have about this investigation and your participation in it. If you have questions you may ask now or you can call us, Drs. Gordon Asmundson or Heather Hadjistavropoulos, at (555) 555–5555. If you are calling long distance, please call collect. If you have any questions about your rights as a research participant, or if you would like to discuss your participation in this investigation with an independent party, you may contact the Chair of the Regina Health District Research Ethics Committee, at (555) 555–9999.

(Continued)

Illustration 6.1. *(Continued)*

Dr. Gordon J. G. Asmundson and Dr. Heather D. Hadjistavropoulos

Clinical Research and Development

SELECTIVE ATTENTION IN DEPRESSION AND
PANIC DISORDER CONSENT FORM

I, _____, have been informed of the nature of this investigation and freely consent to participate in it. A copy of the Information for Potential Participants and this Consent Form have been provided to me.

I understand that my participation is fully voluntary and that I may decide not to participate or to withdraw at any time after agreeing to participate without any consequences to my current or future treatment. I understand that information gained from this investigation is confidential and may be shared only with members of the research team. I also understand that this information will be used for research purposes only and that any details that may reveal my identity will be excluded from research reports and presentations. If some important information regarding my condition becomes known as a result of participating in this investigation, I may give written permission to the researchers to share it with my treatment provider.

I will receive a $30 honorarium to help pay for travel and other expenses that may result from my participation.

If I have any questions regarding the investigation, I can contact Drs. Gordon Asmundson or Heather Hadjistavropoulos at (555) 555–5555. If I have any questions about my rights as a research participant, or if I wish to discuss my participation in this investigation with an independent party, I can contact the Chair of the Regina Health District Research Ethics Committee, at (555) 555–9999.

Participant's Signature: _____

Investigator's Signature: _____

Witness's Signature: _____

Date: _____

participants deal with, control, or overcome the symptoms of their condition? If these types of benefits are likely, state them. If they aren't, be explicit (e.g., "There may not be any direct benefit to you personally from participating in this study") rather than try to avoid the issue.

As for risks and discomforts, you should make every effort to describe these as fully as possible. Of course, studies vary in their inherent degree of risk and discomfort. Some will involve no known risks, and the only discomfort will be the time required to participate (yes, we include giving up personal time as a potential discomfort). Others may involve procedures that stress the participant physically or psychologically, invasive testing, forgoing standard treatment, and the like. Although identifying all potential risks is not always possible, assurance must be given that known risks have been considered.

Confidentiality. It is the researcher's responsibility to ensure the privacy of potential participants and to maintain the confidentiality of the data they provide. There are some general statements regarding confidentiality that you can include as a guarantee in this regard. For example, it is standard to say something like,

> Any information derived from your participation will be strictly confidential. It will be viewed only by members of the research team and will not be shared with any other parties except as may be required by law (e.g., members of the Research Ethics Board, representatives of the Federal Drug Administration). Any details that might reveal your identity will be excluded from our data files and from research reports.

This type of statement is adequate in most cases.

There are instances, perhaps many in clinical research, when more detail is required in the guarantee of confidentiality. Indeed, there is certain information that may come to light that the researcher can't, either by law or personal morals, keep confidential. In particular, studies that might reveal information about abusive relationships, criminal behavior, AIDS or other previously unidentified disease states, and suicidal intent or other significant psychopathologies require more elaborate statements. In these cases, we recommend that you clearly identify the circumstances under which you will be likely to have to break confidentiality. In a related vein, in nontreatment studies of vulnerable populations, we recommend that you obtain specific permission from the participant to share important clinical information that becomes available during the study with their primary care provider.

Voluntary Participation. Consent must not only be informed but also completely voluntary. Inclusion of this section allows you to state explicitly that potential participants do not have to participate if they don't want to, and that they are free to withdraw without any action against them (e.g., withholding treatment) if they decide to do so for any reason after enrolling in a study.

Coercion and Remuneration. Consent must be given freely and without coercion. Improperly induced or pressured consent through excessive remuneration, provision of privileges, or withdrawal of benefits is ethically unacceptable. That is not to say that participants can't be reimbursed for the personal time and effort that it takes them to partake in your study. Payment for time and expenses (such as parking, gas, etc.) is acceptable, as is an offer to provide treatment services (quite common in clinical research) or the provision of small gifts (e.g., giving a gift certificate for Kraft products to the participants of the Peanut Butter Study). As a rule, any remuneration must not be perceived as disproportionate to the requirements of participating. We recommend providing information about remuneration on the Information and Consent Form in all cases where remuneration is offered.

Offer to Answer Questions and Contact Information. It is a good idea to encourage potential participants to ask questions. They may, for any number of reasons, be reluctant to do so spontaneously. Including a written invitation to ask questions, along with a verbal offer and a few specific questions about the study (as we suggested above), is a convenient and easy way of ensuring that a potential participant understands what it is you are asking of him or her. And, because questions about the study may arise at any time, it is essential to provide contact information for the research team and for the chair of your IRB.

Signatures. At minimum, the participant (or legal designate) and researcher need to sign the Information and Consent Form. There may, depending on the nature of your study and the requirements of your IRB, be other signatures that you need to obtain.

Other Information. Above, we have presented the basic information that is required in most Information and Consent Forms. We have not been exhaustive in possibilities. We recommend including a statement like, "A summary of the study, once complete, will be provided to you" along with information of how the summary will be made available. Your IRB may require other information; so, as a rule, check with them.

A Word on Data Fabrication

No discussion on research ethics would be complete without mention of one of the fundamentals of research—fabricating data is contrary to the purpose of the scientific approach and is *absolutely* unacceptable. Still, there are some researchers who partake in this unethical behavior. As we mentioned in Chapter 2, there are many reasons that people get involved in clinical research. Some of these reasons—the joy of discovery and quenching curiosity not being among them—have led some researchers (if we dare call them that) to make up data, sometimes even entire studies, that support their ideas. Why? There is no simple answer, but quite likely, in a general sense they forget that one of their obligations as a researcher is to discover new knowledge, not to make it up. It is appropriate to mention here that null findings, despite not lending ammunition to support your ideas, are valuable and, although sometimes difficult to publish, do make important contributions to our knowledge base. Fabricating data, in addition to very likely ending one's career, leads astray the process of accumulating knowledge based on systematic observation.

Summary

Clinical research is a means to the ultimate end of buttressing existing knowledge in an effort to help people deal with, or overcome, a given set of symptoms. In the pursuit of new knowledge, we need to ensure that the rights of our research participants are not violated and that the potential for harm is minimized. Understanding the principles of research ethics, being vigilant and responsive to these principles within the context of any given research method, having a firm grasp of research methods, and being in close communication with others (e.g., an IRB, mentor, colleagues) can assist researchers in this regard.

References

Bersoff, D. M., & Bersoff, D. N. (1999). Ethical perspectives in clinical research. In P. C. Kendall, J. N. Butcher, & G. N. Holmbeck (Eds.), *Handbook of research methods in clinical psychology* (2nd ed., pp. 31–53). New York: John Wiley.

Canadian Psychological Association. (1991). *Canadian code of ethics for psychologists.* Ottawa: Author.

Hadjistavropoulos, T., & Malloy, D. C. (2000). Making ethical choices: A comprehensive decision-making model for Canadian psychologists. *Canadian Psychology, 41,* 104–115.

Hyman, S. (1999). Protecting patients, preserving progress: Ethics in mental health illness research. *Academic Medicine, 74,* 258–259.

Koocher, G. P., & Keith-Spiegel, P. (1998). *Ethics in psychology: Professional standards and cases.* New York: Oxford University Press.

Mann, T. (1994). Informed consent for psychological research: Do subjects comprehend consent forms and understand their legal rights? *Psychological Science, 5,* 140–143.

Michels, R. (1999). Are research ethics boards bad for our mental health? *New England Journal of Medicine, 340,* 1427–1430.

Roberts, L. W., & Roberts, B. (1999). Psychiatric research ethics: An overview of guidelines and current ethical dilemmas in the study of mental illness. *Biological Psychiatry, 46,* 1025–1038.

White, R. M. (2000). Unraveling the Tuskegee study of untreated syphilis. *Archives of Internal Medicine, 160,* 585–598.

PART II

Data and Methods

7

Understanding Data

A psychiatrist once said to us, "I love working with people who have Obsessive Compulsive Disorder, they are never late for appointments." We asked her if people with other disorders are less reliable in showing up for appointments. She decided to find out. She started recording how late clients were for their appointments. She found that people with Obsessive Compulsive Disorder were indeed less likely to be late for appointments when compared to her clients who had Major Depressive Disorder. The datum (singular for data) was how many minutes her clients were late for their appointments. This little vignette shows that data can be almost anything that you can measure. That is the key—measurability. If you can measure something reliably, you can use it as data for research purposes. That is, of course, if the data are also valid.

The purpose of this chapter is to describe what constitutes data for research purposes. We will review the following:

1. The various ways in which we can determine if a measure is reliable

2. What the concept of validity means

3. The various types of data that are most commonly used in clinical research

Reliability

A measure can be considered reliable if what is measured can produce the same results again and again. For example, if we wanted to see if frequency of eye-blinks predicts truthfulness, we could have several people intentionally tell us stories where they either lie or tell the truth. We would, of course, not know who was lying or telling the truth. Lying and truth-telling would be determined by someone other than those who were measuring eye-blinks. If the people measuring eye-blinks knew who was lying or telling the truth, this might produce bias in their records. They might, for example, unintentionally "see" more eye-blinks among liars. We will discuss problems of bias in detail in Chapter 8. For the present, let's understand that biases and other uncontrolled factors (called extraneous variables) can contaminate our results in unpredictable ways.

After we have had someone select our liars and truth-tellers, we would record the number of times each person blinked during a given period of time. For convenience, let's say that we videotaped our participants while they were telling their stories. Now, we can test the reliability of our measures of eye-blinks. In this case, we can do it in several ways. First, we could compare your counts with mine. If we recorded similar numbers of eye-blinks per given unit of time (say one minute), we could consider our data to be reliable. Or, one of us could record the number of eye-blinks at one point in time and then record the eye-blinks after reviewing the videotape at another time. If the number of eye-blinks recorded at time 1 was similar to those recorded at time 2, we could assume our data were reliable.

Each of the above measures of reliability has a different name. The first measure of reliability is called inter-rater reliability, whereas the second is called inter-interval reliability. There are also other measures of reliability, and we discuss these below.

Inter-Rater Reliability

Inter-rater reliability is established when two independent raters record the same data. Let's look at an example of how we might establish inter-rater reliability of a measure of aggressiveness in children. Some years back, one of us (G. R. N.) was training students to assess aggressive behavior in a group of hearing-impaired children. A special class based on behavior modification principles had been set up for 10 emotionally disturbed children, and two students had been hired to help the teacher apply consequences for both appropriate and inappropriate behaviors. One of the biggest problems was that the children behaved in very aggressive ways toward each other and the teacher. The teacher, the students, and the consulting psychologist observed the children for several days and identified a series of aggressive acts such as hitting, biting, and spitting that were frequent and very disruptive to the class. We then carefully defined, using specific classes of behaviors, exactly what we meant by hitting, biting, and so on. Then, to determine if our definitions were reliable, the two students independently recorded each aggressive act for each child. We had devised a special coding form that had each child's name at the top and time in minutes down the side. After a 30-minute observation period, we compared the number of aggressive acts recorded by the two observers. We found that more than 90% of the aggressive acts recorded by observer A were also recorded by observer B. This was an acceptable level of inter-rater reliability (in fact, anything over .80 is generally acceptable), and it showed that our definitions of aggressive behavior could be accurately observed and recorded.

Inter-Interval Reliability

Inter-interval reliability is established when the same rater obtains data from the same data sample at two different points in time. In order to obtain inter-interval reliability, we must have a video, audio, or other type of record of the measured event. Inter-interval reliability is the type of reliability that is, for example, obtained after an election and the vote count is challenged. When the votes are recounted, we are establishing the reliability of the original count. We count them twice to determine the accuracy of the original vote count.

Test-Retest Reliability

Another common measure of reliability is called test-retest reliability. To obtain test-retest reliability we measure our variable (see Chapter 9 for a discussion of variables) at one point in time and then remeasure it once again at another point in time. Although this seems to be the same thing as inter-interval reliability, it is actually different. In test-retest reliability we independently measure our variable at two different times, whereas for inter-interval reliability we assess the same measurement of our variable at two different times. In our above example, we recorded videotaped eye-blinks at two times. It was the same event that we measured. If we wanted to obtain a measure of test-retest reliability of eye-blinks when people were lying or telling the truth, we would measure the eye-blink rate of each of our participants at time 1. We would then have them repeat their story (or tell another) at a later time, under the same conditions (e.g., lying or telling the truth) and again measure their rate of blinking.

Summary

There are other measures of reliability, but the three discussed above are the types that are most commonly used to determine if *a variable is being*

Illustration 7.1. Three Main Types of Reliability

Type	How to Assess
Inter-rater	Have two (or more) independent raters record the same data during a single observational session and assess correspondence.
Inter-interval	Have a single rater assess data from a single data collection session at two different points in time and assess correspondence.
Test-Retest	Measure a variable during data collection period, remeasure it during another data collection period at a later point in time, and assess correspondence.

meaured reliably. These three common measures of reliability are summarized in Illustration 7.1. For now, we need only to remember that our data must be reliable if we are to use them for research purposes. Regardless of the specific method used, we obtain our estimate of reliability by comparing our records. Typically we do this by correlating one record with another. If our correlation coefficient is approximately .80 or higher, we can be fairly confident that our data are reliable. Correlational procedures are described in Chapter 10.

Validity

A measure must not only be reliable, it must also be valid. Validity means that the measure we are using is truly tapping into the construct being measured. We might, for example, find that depressed people *repeatedly* report that they feel tired in the afternoon. Although this might be a reliable measure, does it assess the construct of depression? Probably not. Although many depressed people are tired in the afternoon, they would likely report being tired in the morning and evening as well. In addition, many people who are not depressed will also report afternoon tiredness. The concept of validity is of utmost importance—it is only through use of a valid measure that we can be certain we are accurately measuring what we claim to be measuring. The concept is also complex; let's take a moment to look at several ways in which we can assess whether a measure is valid.

Face Validity

From a technical point of view, face validity isn't a true measure of validity. It is simply based on appearance—does the measure appear to measure the construct we are interested in. For example, if we developed a questionnaire to measure sibling rivalry in children, questions such as, "Do you think your mother likes your brother/sister more than you?" might appear to measure the construct. If so, then we would say that the items have face validity. However, in order to determine if, in fact, the items are valid, we must use more psychometrically sound determinations of validity.

Construct Validity

Construct validity is a concept that refers to the extent to which a measure reflects the construct of interest. In order to determine construct validity we usually have to use some of the other measures of validity described below. Construct validity is determined by assessing how well a measure corresponds to other measures and domains associated with the construct. For example, if we want to measure the construct of anxiety, we would have to determine what anxiety is and, thereafter, assess how well our measure corresponded to theories of anxiety and to established measures of anxiety. Look at the next three ways of determining validity and you will better understand construct validity, as they can all be used to determine if a measure has construct validity.

Concurrent Validity

Concurrent validity is determined by assessing how well a measure corresponds to another measure or criterion obtained at the same time. For example, if we want to determine the concurrent validity of a new measure of anxiety, we might have participants complete the new measure along with an established measure of anxiety. If the participants' scores on the new measure generally corresponded to their scores on the established measure, we would have evidence of concurrent validity. If scores on the new measure correlated with those on *several* established measures of anxiety, we would be even more convinced of its concurrent validity.

Predictive Validity

Predictive validity refers to how well a measure obtained at one point in time correlates with another measure or criterion in the future. For example, there is evidence that a measure of fear of anxiety symptoms, the Anxiety Sensitivity Index (ASI; Reiss, Peterson, Gursky, & McNally, 1985), is a good predictor of who does or does not develop Panic Disorder. Schmidt and colleagues (Schmidt, Lerew, & Jackson, 1997), in a recent study using army recruits, gave the ASI to a large number of men and women who were entering the armed forces. They then determined which of these people developed spontaneous panic attacks at a later time. Those who had high scores on the ASI (but not necessarily higher scores on other measures) were much more likely to develop such attacks than were those who had lower scores. Thus, the ASI was a valid predictor of spontaneous panic attacks.

Convergent and Discriminant Validity

We include convergent and discriminant validity under the same heading because they are really opposite sides of a coin. Convergent validity is a form of concurrent validity that is especially meaningful when paired with discriminant validity. As we have seen, concurrent (and convergent) validity is determined when a measure of interest correlates highly with established measures of the construct that are given at the same time. That is, we would expect a new measure, if valid, to correlate highly with established criteria.

Discriminant validity is just the opposite. If a new measure is a valid measure of our construct, then we would not expect it to correlate highly with measures of unrelated constructs. For example, if we had a questionnaire that we hoped would be a valid measure of, say, fear of pain, we would not expect our questionnaire to be positively correlated with unrelated constructs such as social competency or state anxiety.

If a new measure has high convergent validity and high discriminant validity, we can be quite sure that it is highly valid. In other words, it has demonstrated construct validity.

Summary

Like reliability, there are several different types of validity. It is only through careful consideration of each of the types of validity (see Illustration 7.2) that we can ascertain that we are accurately measuring what we claim to be measuring.

Types of Data

Okay, now let's get back to our discussion of data. We can conceptualize two kinds of data—*quantitative* and *qualitative*. These terms are similar to, but technically different from, *objective* and *subjective*. Quantitative data are data that can be objectively measured. That is, they can be counted and do not require interpretation. For example, eye-blinks would constitute

Illustration 7.2.   Types of Validity

Type	How to Assess
Face	Ask the question, "Does the measure appear to measure what it is supposed to measure?"
Construct	Assess how well the measure corresponds to other measures and domains associated with the same construct.
Concurrent and Convergent	Assess how well the measure corresponds to another measure or criterion of the same construct obtained at the same time.
Predictive	Assess how well the measure obtained at one point in time correlates with another measure or criterion of the same or similar construct in the future.
Discriminant	Assess the degree to which the measure corresponds to other measures or criteria of unrelated constructs obtained at the same time. In this case, low correspondence implies high validity.

quantitative data if we carefully define what we mean by an eye-blink. If we define an eye-blink as "both eye lids must touch and the period of time they touch must be less than one second," then we can reliably measure each eye-blink. We can count them. Similarly, if we have a person take the Beck Depression Inventory (Beck, Ward, Mendelson, Mock, & Erbaugh, 1961), a reliable measure of depression, we can total the scores for each item and get a quantitative measure of depression. As you can see, quantitative data are data that can be easily measured and do not require interpretation. Most of the data that we collect are quantitative. Because most research uses quantitative data, we will focus most of our attention on these types of data. However, before we do so, let's take a look at what is meant by qualitative data.

Qualitative Data

Sometimes data we are interested in may not be easily counted (or, in other words, quantified). For example, suppose a counselor has her clients keep daily journals because she is interested in assessing changes in negative affect of her clients over time. To do this, she might compare the frequency of negative affect statements to positive affect statements that are made in the journals. This would be very hard to measure in a quantitative way. Negative and positive affect could be expressed in a variety of ways. In order to assess negative and positive affect, the counselor would have to establish rules of what constitutes a statement of negative or positive affect. For example, she might define negative affect as any sentence that included the phrases "I feel sad," "I am depressed," "I am bored," and so on. Positive affect statements might include phrases such as "I feel good," "I am enjoying life," and "I'm happy." Once these rules are defined, the counselor could record the frequency of each type of statement. Or, she could determine whether each sentence was a "neutral," "negative affect," or "positive affect" sentence. Ideally, she would have a second, knowledgeable person evaluate the same sentences to determine the reliability of the categories.

Notice that qualitative data require subjective decisions as to what constitutes an instance of datum. This does not mean that the data are not measurable or are necessarily unreliable. As our example shows, we can measure affect or other subjective variables, but that which we are measuring is not easily counted without establishing appropriate rules and categories.

Another example of qualitative data and research might be useful to clarify the differences between quantitative and qualitative data. One of the authors, G. R. N., a clinical psychologist, believes (as do most mental health workers) that we must do more than relieve a client's problems. We should also try to increase the client's enjoyment of life. This lead to a series of studies on the concept of "fun." His ultimate goal was to find ways to increase the levels of fun people experienced. To do this he had to identify what people meant by "fun." He asked various groups of people to fill out several open-ended statements such as "I really have fun when I . . . ," and "The most fun I've ever had was when I . . . ."

From the responses he tried to identify meaningful and coherent concepts of what people meant by fun. This required extracting concepts from very differently worded responses. In order to ensure that his categories were consistently extracted, he developed several rules for establishing categories. He then had a research assistant go through the responses using his category rules to see if she obtained the same information. As with many studies using qualitative data, there was a lot of fine-tuning done on the categories. The original categories were changed several times as different patterns appeared. The purpose of these studies was not to count the ways in which people have fun, but simply to identify common areas of fun experienced by various individuals.

With some types of qualitative data we can eventually analyze the data using statistics, but this is not always the case. Fortunately, there are other methods for evaluating qualitative data. These methods are beyond the scope of the current book, but there are several good books, such as the *Handbook of Qualitative Research* (Denzin & Lincoln, 1994), that describe these methods.

Quantitative Data

By far, most research uses quantitative data. We can conceptualize most quantitative data as falling into three categories—self-report, behavioral, and physiological (Rachman & Hodgson, 1974). These are broad categories, but generally encompass most of the types of data collected by those doing clinical research. Each of these three types of data sample different domains and can be used for different purposes.

Self-Report Data. Self-report data are based on what people say about themselves. Self-reports often access information that is not readily available from other sources. For example, we might ask people to tell us if they are experiencing a headache. Although we might observe a person to see if he or she is grimacing, many may not show obvious discomfort. We are also unlikely to determine if a person is experiencing a headache using physiological measures. Besides, observation and physiological measures can be time-consuming and expensive. So why not just ask the person? Self-report data are easy to obtain and require little time and expense.

Behavioral Data. Behavioral data are obtained by measuring what a person does. For example, if we are interested in what people of different backgrounds do in their leisure time, we could observe them and record the activities they engage in. Or, in the case of the headache sufferer noted above, we might observe the extent to which he or she grimaces, solicits assistance, or avoids certain stimuli or activities.

Physiological Data. Physiological data are obtained by measuring various biological activities of the person. When you last went to your physician and she did a blood test, she was obtaining physiological data. As with self-report and behavioral data, there are many types of physiological data that are used by clinical researchers. For example, in one of our studies (Stein & Asmundson, 1994) we had patients and control participants do various tasks, all the while measuring heart rate, blood pressure, respiratory frequency, end-tidal (expired) CO^2, and plasma epinephrine and norepinephrine levels with the purpose of seeing if the groups differed in their data points as a result of the tasks.

Comparing Sources of Quantitative Data. The three types of data described above may or may not produce similar results. For example, Rachman and Hodgson (1974) have shown that self-reports, behavioral measures, and physiological measures of fear may be discordant. A person might state that she (or he) is fearful of snakes, but still approach and pick up a snake. Similarly, a person may deny being afraid of snakes, but show marked increases in heart rate when approaching a snake. This kind of discordance, according to Rachman and Hodgson, typically occurs when fear levels are moderate. When fear is very mild or intense, we are more likely to see all three measures showing the same pattern of fear.

Because of problems of discordance of measures, costs of obtaining data, and the purposes for which the data will be used, you must carefully consider which types of quantitative data best suit your purposes. Below, we describe self-report data in greater detail and provide examples of the things that need to be considered in selecting a particular self-report data source. Although we do not go into detail here, similar decisions apply when selecting measures of behavioral and physiological data.

Self-Report Data

We obtain self-report data whenever we ask people to answer questions about themselves or events in their lives. Self-report data are probably the most common type of data obtained by mental health researchers. The ways in which we obtain self-report data can vary markedly. For example, many mental health researchers use a semi-structured interview such as the Structured Clinical Interview for DSM-III-R (SCID; Spitzer, Williams, Gibbon, & First, 1992) and its recent revisions or the Anxiety Disorders Interview Schedule (ADIS; DiNardo, Brown, & Barlow, 1994) to obtain psychiatric diagnoses for people in psychological distress.

Semi-Structured Interviews

Semi-structured interviews are used by trained clinicians who ask specific questions of the person being interviewed. These instruments are "semi-structured" rather than fully structured, because there are times that the person doing the interview must depart from the exact content of the interview to clarify a person's answer. The questions used in semi-structured clinical interviews are typically answered with a yes/no (binary) response to specific questions. For example, if the clinician is assessing the person for Posttraumatic Stress Disorder, he or she would ask the person questions such as, "At any time during your life have you ever been involved in a natural disaster, a physical assault, a serious accident, or a war, or have you seen seriously injured or dead people?" and, if so, "In the last six months, have any of these events kept coming back to you in some way, perhaps in your thoughts or dreams?" (Spitzer et al., 1992). In the hands of trained individuals, semi-structured interviews provide reliable and valid diagnoses based on criteria established in the *Diagnostic and Statistical Manual for Mental Disorders* (American Psychiatric Association, 1968, 1980, 1987, 1994, 2000).

Semi-structured interviews are available for many types of disorders and problems. For example, we have used a semi-structured interview for assessing functional gastrointestinal disorders (Norton, Norton, Asmundson, Thompson, & Larsen, 1999). This interview (as with the interviews for determining psychiatric disorders) was developed by specialists from around the world. And, like those used for psychiatric disorders, it is undergoing constant modifications as we obtain new information about the nature of the disorders.

Semi-structured interviews, although very useful for obtaining diagnoses for a wide range of problems, are often very time-consuming. For example, if a person uses the full SCID (Spitzer et al., 1992) for assessing *DSM* disorders, the interview may take several hours. This can be a very expensive way to obtain data.

Paper-and-Pencil Measures

An alternative to using a semi-structured interview to obtain information about various disorders would be to use many of the reliable and valid paper-and-pencil measures. Paper-and-pencil measures are available for a wide variety of domains. For example, there are measures of psychopathology (e.g., Minnesota Multiphasic Personality Inventory—2 [Hathaway & McKinley, 1989]; Beck Depression Inventory [Beck et al., 1961]); personality (e.g., Revised NEO Personality Inventory [Costa & McCrae, 1992]; Anxiety Sensitivity Index [Reiss et al., 1985]); and so on. Some paper-and-pencil inventories assess a wide variety of domains. For example, the Minnesota Multiphasic Personality Inventory provides the examiner with measures of psychopathology, such as depression, and measures of personality disorders, such as antisocial personality disorder. Other paper-and-pencil measures focus on single domains, such as depression.

The most frequently used instrument for measuring depression is the Beck Depression Inventory (Beck et al., 1961). This is a 21-item test that can be administered to an individual or group of people in a brief period of time. The instructions are contained in the test, and it is very easy for persons taking the test to circle answers that best describe their current state. There are thousands of such tests that have been carefully researched to establish their reliability, validity, and ease of use. Information about many of the paper-and-pencil tests used by mental health workers can be obtained in the yearly publication of *Mental Measurements Handbook* (e.g., Buros, 1980) or similar resource materials, including *Commissioned Reviews of 250 Psychological Tests* (Maltby, Lewis, & Hill, 2000) and *Measures for Clinical Practice* (Corcoran & Fischer, 2000). Although there are numerous paper-and-pencil measures available to us, we should be careful which ones we select to be used as data. There are several reasons for this. First, not all measures have been carefully developed and may have poor or unknown reliability and validity. Second, even if an instrument has been shown to be reliable and valid for one group, this doesn't necessarily mean it is valid for other groups. For example, instruments that have been developed with adult samples may not provide valid results with children. Third, even though two tests purport to measure the same domain, they may not. For example, the Beck Anxiety Inventory (Beck, Epstein, Brown, & Steer, 1988) has been shown to be primarily a measure of "panic-like anxiety symptoms" (Cox, Cohen, Direnfeld, & Swinson, 1996). Finally, although two instruments may measure the same domain, one may be used infrequently by researchers. There are many advantages for using not only well-established measures, but also for using measures that are frequently used by others. The primary advantage is ease of comparison of results. If researchers at several different centers obtain similar results, we can be more confident that our data are valid.

Idiosyncratic Situations

Other data can be obtained without the use of formal measures. Sometimes the data of interest to us may be unique to our situation and circumstances. For example, we described in the section on inter-rater reliability a project where students were recording aggressive behavior. At that time, there was no well-established coding form for aggressive behaviors. They had to create their own. Similarly, within the domain of physiological data, technology daily gives us new measures that denote important physiological function. When we were interested in collecting data about functioning of the vagus nerve in patients with various psychopathologies, we had to hire an engineer to help develop an interface between the EKG and computer technologies of the time. Today, computerized (and portable) machines dedicated to measuring this type of data are readily available.

It is sometimes the case in clinical research that we have to establish our own, unique measures. This is perfectly acceptable as long as we establish the reliability and validity of the measure before it is used for data purposes. But, as we have stated before, you should use well-established measures when they are available.

Summary

In this chapter we have described various sources of data. We strongly emphasized that whatever type of data you use and however you obtain them, they must be reliable and valid. We described several ways of ensuring your data are reliable. We also described various ways in which you can ensure that your data are valid. In clinical research most forms of data will be obtained using self-report measures, behavioral measures, or physiological measures. Because much of the research done by clinical investigators involves self-report data, we have provided detailed information on several methods for obtaining this kind of data. The bottom line is that almost anything is a potential data source, assuming it can be measured reliably and is a valid indicator of the construct you are interested in.

References

American Psychiatric Association. (1968). *Diagnostic and statistical manual of mental disorders* (2nd ed.). Washington, DC: Author.

American Psychiatric Association. (1980). *Diagnostic and statistical manual of mental disorders* (3rd ed.). Washington, DC: Author.

American Psychiatric Association. (1987). *Diagnostic and statistical manual of mental disorders* (3rd ed., rev.). Washington, DC: Author.

American Psychiatric Association. (1994). *Diagnostic and statistical manual of mental disorders* (4th ed.). Washington, DC: Author.

American Psychiatric Association. (2000). *Diagnostic and statistical manual of mental disorders* (4th ed., text rev.). Washington, DC: Author.

Beck, A. T., Epstein, N., Brown, G., & Steer, R. A. (1988). An inventory for measuring clinical anxiety: Psychometric properties. *Journal of Consulting and Clinical Psychology, 56,* 893–897.

Beck, A. T., Ward, C. H., Mendelson, M., Mock, J., & Erbaugh, J. (1961). An inventory for measuring depression. *Archives of General Psychiatry, 4,* 561–571.

Buros, O. K. (Ed.). (1980). *10th mental measurements handbook.* Highland Park, NJ: Gryphon Press.

Corcoran, K. J., & Fischer, J. (Eds.). (2000). *Measures for clinical practice* (3rd ed.). Portland, OR: Portland State University.

Costa, P. T., & McCrae, R. R. (1992). *Revised NEO Personality Inventory NEO-PI-R and NEO Five-Factor Inventory (NEO-FFI) professional manual.* Odessa, FL: Psychological Assessment Resources.

Cox, B. J., Cohen, E., Direnfeld, D. M., & Swinson, R. P. (1996). Does the Beck Anxiety Inventory measure anything beyond panic attack symptoms? *Behaviour Research and Therapy, 34,* 949–954.

Denzin, N. K., & Lincoln, Y. S. (1994). *The handbook of qualitative research.* Thousand Oaks, CA: Sage.

DiNardo, P., Brown, T. A., & Barlow, D. H. (1994). *Anxiety disorders interview schedule for DSM-IV.* New York: Graywind.

Hathaway, S. R., & McKinley, J. C. (1989). *Minnesota Multiphasic Personality Inventory-2: Manual for administration.* Minneapolis: University of Minnesota Press.

Maltby, J., Lewis, C. A., & Hill, A. P. (2000). *Commissioned reviews on 250 psychological tests.* Wales, UK: Edwin Mellen Press.

Norton, G. R., Norton, P. J., Asmundson, G. J. G., Thompson, L. A., & Larsen, D. K. (1999). Neurotic butterflies in my stomach: The role of anxiety, anxiety sensitivity and depression in functional gastrointestinal disorders. *Journal of Psychosomatic Research, 47,* 233–240.

Rachman, S., & Hodgson, R. I. (1974). Synchrony and desynchrony in fear and avoidance. *Behaviour Research and Therapy, 12,* 311–318.

Reiss, S., Peterson, R. A., Gursky, D. M., & McNally, R. J. (1986). Anxiety sensitivity, injury sensitivity, and individual differences in fearfulness. *Behaviour Research and Therapy, 26,* 341–345.

Schmidt, N. B., Lerew, D. R., & Jackson, R. J. (1997). The role of anxiety sensitivity in the pathogenesis of panic: Prospective evaluations of spontaneous panic attacks during acute stress. *Journal of Abnormal Psychology, 106,* 355–364.

Spitzer, R. L., Williams, J. B. W., Gibbon, M., & First, M. (1992). The Structured Clinical Interview for the DSM-III-R (SCID). I: History, rationale, and description. *Archives of General Psychiatry, 49,* 624–629.

Stein, M. B., & Asmundson, G. J. G. (1994). Autonomic function in Panic Disorder: Cardiorespiratory and plasmacatecholamine responsivity to multiple challenges of the autonomic nervous system. *Biological Psychiatry, 36,* 548–558.

8

Guidelines for Collecting Sound Data

In Chapter 7 we described various types of data. In this chapter, we describe how data are collected. For many researchers this is the most enjoyable and rewarding part of doing research. However, data collection can, at times, require a great deal of ingenuity. To some extent this relates to the specific type of research method that the researcher employs. For example, a survey method is generally more straightforward than are quasi-experimental or true experimental designs.

Our purpose here is to provide some general guidelines for collecting data that apply across different research methods. Application of these guidelines should, we hope, increase the confidence you have in your findings. They should also increase the likelihood that others (researchers and clinicians) will accept your findings. We focus on using measures that are reliable and valid. We stress the importance of using measures that are generally accepted by people in your field. We also describe some of the most common experimental biases that can occur during research and compromise the soundness of your data.

General Guidelines for Collecting Data

The guidelines we present are just that—guidelines. They are presented to assist you in making good decisions about what type of data to collect and how to collect them. They may be especially useful for those of you who have not done much research or for those who have not done research for some time and need a bit of a refresher.

There are three general guidelines we feel are most important.

1. Select reliable, valid, and commonly used measures for obtaining your data.

2. Reduce experimental biases that might invalidate your findings.

3. Choose an appropriate research method.

Let's look at each of these in more detail.

Selecting Measures

In Chapter 7 we introduced the concepts of reliability and validity. Recall that reliability has to do with repeatability. That is, two people collecting the same information should get the same or similar results, or you should get similar results if you collect the same data at two different time periods. Validity refers to obtaining data that accurately reflect the construct you are measuring. For example, if you are interested in depression, then the instruments you are using should measure depression and not some other variable.

It is often the case that inexperienced researchers want to, or believe they have to, create a measure to use in their study. This, quite simply, is not typically the case. Probably the two most important reasons for using measures that already exist are that (a) they will likely have been carefully researched and their reliability and validity for various groups will have been established, and (b) you will be better able to compare your finding with those of other researchers. If we use new measures or ones that are not frequently used, we may have difficulty showing that our findings are similar to those obtained by other researchers. Although there are methods for comparing results from different measures, they are quite time-consuming and require fairly sophisticated statistics.

It is easy to become seduced by measures that seem to be "cutting edge" or tap into "deeper domains" of thinking, feeling, or behaving than do more conventional measures. Recall that if an instrument seems to have the right items to tap into a construct, it is said to have face validity. However, face validity does not mean that the measure necessarily taps into the construct you want to assess. Nor does it mean that the measure is reliable.

Let's look at an example. For many years psychologists, psychiatrists, and other therapists (especially those with a psychodynamic orientation) have used the Rorschach Ink Blot Test to assess putative unconscious forces underlying peoples' feelings, cravings, and actions. The Rorschach consists of a series of generally symmetrical, ambiguous ink blots. They look like someone had placed a blob of ink in the center of a page and folded it with the ink squishing out on both halves.

Persons who are being assessed with the Rorschach are asked to look at the ambiguous figures and to state what they "see." Sometimes people respond to the whole inkblot, sometimes to parts of it. The idea behind projective tests like this is that the person will "project" into the ambiguous figure the content of his or her unconscious mind. This presumably permits the therapist a peek into the irrational forces that drive the person's thoughts, feelings, and actions.

This seems to be a good idea. All too often, however, therapists interpret a person's responses to the inkblots in very different ways. In other words, the inkblot tests are often unreliable. So, in the 1960s a new inkblot test, the Structured Objective Rorschach Test (SORT), was developed to reduce the problems of unreliability. The SORT used a series of multiple choice questions to assess a person's response to each of many inkblots. After looking at each inkblot, the person would circle an answer that best described what he or she saw in the inkblot. Each choice was supposed to be associated with a particular part of the inkblot. Neat! The SORT promised a much more reliable and objective format for assessing unconscious forces.

Unfortunately, further testing indicated that this "sexy" new instrument lacked good reliability. For example, Langer and Norton (1965) administered the SORT to a large number of undergraduate students in the conventional manner—they had each person look at each inkblot and then circle the items that best described what they saw in the inkblots. However, they took it a step farther. They had each participant circle the section of the inkblot that she or he was actually "seeing." The circled parts of the inkblot often bore no relationship to where the makers of the SORT said they should be. The test was not valid.

The importance of this example is in stressing that not all information that looks or sounds good, necessarily is good. Too much pop psychology and medicine are based on what sounds or looks good rather than in good science. So, when you need to select a specific measure or group of measures with which to collect data, spend some time assessing the reliability and validity of the measures within the group that you wish to apply it. In some cases it is appropriate to use single-item measures or behavioral ratings but, once again, care needs to be taken in selecting these. Ultimately, if the measure or measures are not reliable and valid, then very little confidence can be placed in the data collected and the conclusions that stem from them.

All other things being equal, use well-established measures for collecting your data. By doing so, you can be more certain that your measures are

Illustration 8.1.   Important Points to Consider for Collecting Sound Data

1. Make sure you use measures that are reliable. Remember, reliability means "repeatability." That is, you should obtain similar values if you use the measure on two different occasions (assuming nothing has happened between the measurement periods to change the scores), two different people measuring the same construct at the same time should get similar results, and you should get similar results if you evaluate the same data (e.g., videotaped interviews) on two different occasions.

2. Make sure that the instruments you are using are valid. Validity refers to how accurately you are measuring the construct under consideration. For example, if you are interested in assessing depression, does your instrument really measure depression?

3. Except in cases where well-established measures are not available, use measures that are commonly used by others. This will increase the likelihood that you are using reliable and valid measures and will help you and others compare your data to those obtained by other researchers.

reliable and valid. This will also facilitate comparisons of findings. As was pointed out above, when people use very different measures (especially if one of the measures is an obscure or idiosyncratic measure) we can't be sure if we are getting the same magnitude of effect or if we are measuring slightly different constructs. There are, of course, times when measures that are not common are appropriate, or where you may need to create a new measure, but you should think very carefully about when and why this needs to be done. Important points to remember are presented in Illustration 8.1.

Now, let's turn our attention to some other ways in which we might inadvertently contaminate and invalidate the data we collect. We may be very careful to select reliable, valid, and commonly used instruments to collect our data, and then spoil them by allowing experimental biases to creep into the way we collect our data. We discuss two types of common experimental biases—experimenter and participant biases. Sometimes it is difficult to determine if biases have occurred and, if they have, whether they can be best conceptualized as experimenter bias or participant bias. Experimenter and participant biases occur when either the experimenter or the participants do something that distorts the data. The primary difference between these biases is related to who distorts the data. The similarity is that both biases lead to results that would not have occurred if the biases were not present.

Experimenter Biases

Let's illustrate experimenter bias with a couple of examples. For two reasons, these examples are hypothetical. First, it is often very difficult to determine when experimenter biases occur. They are usually unintentional, so we can't easily glean them from research articles and may never actually discover them if they do occur. Second, it would be very tacky to criticize someone for something that was not intentional. Even the most competent researchers can make unintentional mistakes that bias data (this is one reason why replication is so important).

Experimenter bias occurs when the behavior of the researcher influences the outcome of the results. As we stated above, this is usually unintentional. But, sometimes even the simplest differences in the way in which participants are treated can markedly influence the outcome of a study. Experimenter bias can occur in different types of studies. Let's look at a few specific examples.

Comparing Active Treatment to Placebo

The following fictional, but highly probable, vignette is an illustration of how a researcher can unintentionally alter the outcome of a treatment outcome study comparing an active medication to a placebo. This type of experimenter bias is usually referred to as a *demand effect*. That is, the researcher places different demands on different participants.

Let's imagine that you are a medical researcher and you have just developed a new medication to reduce tension headaches. You've gone through all of the regulatory agencies, and you are now ready to test your new compound on humans. You realize that if the product bears out, you stand to make a lot of money. At the same time, you want to make sure your product actually works, so you carefully set up your study. You place an advertisement in the newspaper and solicit participants. You select 100 participants who clearly have tension headaches (and not migraines or other nontension types of headaches) and you then randomly assign them into your treatment and control groups. The participants in the treatment group are those who receive the medication, and those in the control group get an inactive placebo. To make sure you know which group each participant is assigned to you put a red sticker on the folders of those receiving your new medication and a blue sticker on the folders of those receiving the placebo.

Each participant is asked to come into your office once a week for an evaluation. When they visit, you obtain information about how many headaches they have had during the previous week and how severe each of them was.

You also ask each person a series of questions designed to identify whether he or she has been having any side effects. This goes on for 8 weeks.

You notice that with each passing week the participants assigned your medication are reporting fewer and fewer headaches. As well, you notice that the severity of headaches in the medication group has diminished since the beginning of the study. You are, of course, thrilled. It looks like you have a product that is effective in reducing both the frequency and severity of headaches. You are also starting to see the dollar signs.

You have committed a severe experimenter bias error and your results are totally invalid. What was your error? It is one of the most common experimenter errors—you knew who was taking the medication and who was taking the placebo. Why is this such a big deal? Well, you are hoping the medication pans out because it will help alleviate the suffering of your patients and, to boot, it will bring you fame and fortune. The desire to succeed could easily (albeit unintentionally) affect the way in which you interact with the participants in each of the groups.

Even subtle differences could cause participants to give you different reports on how well they are doing. For example, Ms. Casey, that nice lady with the lovely 2-year-old twins, noticed that you seemed very pleased when, on her third visit, she reported fewer headaches. "Well," she thought, "if my doctor is pleased, I must be getting better." On the other hand, when Mr. Brodsky was in for his third visit and reported that he was doing better, he noticed that you looked dismayed. "Wow," he thought, "I don't think the doctor thinks I'm doing so well. If that's the case, I must not have improved. After all, the doctor knows more about this than I do."

The subtle differences in your behavior may have created changes in each participant's beliefs about the effectiveness of the treatment and could have changed how they perceived their headaches. In the first case, Ms. Casey may ignore a slight headache or attribute it to something else, such as not having slept well the night before. Mr. Brodsky may do just the opposite. He may begin to exaggerate the severity of his headaches.

How could you have prevented these possible differences in demand characteristics? One way would have been to use a double-blind experimental design. Correctly, you didn't let the participants know whether they were receiving the medication or the placebo—they were kept "blind." Doing this reduced the likelihood that a participant might respond differently because of knowing he or she was receiving the active medication. A participant's expectation of getting better as a result of knowingly receiving the active medication is a form of a subtle demand that can influence behavior. This is also true of a person knowingly receiving the placebo, except the subtle demand relates to getting worse and reporting more frequent and severe headaches.

You could also have taken the "blind" process one step farther. Because you knew which type of medication your participants were on (because of the color-coded files), you unintentionally influenced the way they reported headache severity and frequency. In order to eliminate this type of demand effect, you could have kept yourself "blind," or ignorant, of who was on medication and who was on placebo. In this case, the only person who would know whether a participant was receiving medication or placebo would be the pharmacist who made the tablets. This person would randomly assign the participants to the groups but would not have any direct contact with them or with you. In this way the pharmacist can't influence the outcome of the study. Nor can you.

In summary, if there are two important groups in treatment studies—the researchers and the participants—and if we keep knowledge of who is receiving which treatment from one group, then we have a single-blind study. If we keep both groups from having knowledge of who is receiving which treatment, then we have a double-blind study. A double-blind study is less likely to produce demand effects than is a single-blind study.

It is important to understand that we may never be able to eliminate demand effects completely. All we can do is try to reduce them as much as possible. For example, even if we use a double-blind procedure when comparing medication and placebo, as in the headache study described above, there still may be factors that lead either the researcher or the participant to believe that a given participant is receiving the medication or the placebo. Most medications have side effects, such as the dry mouth produced by some antidepressants. If, in a study comparing an antidepressant with a placebo, some of the participants report dry mouth, either the participant or the researcher might assume they are receiving the medication and not the placebo. This might influence the participant's or the researcher's beliefs, which, in turn, might influence the outcome of the study.

Comparing Two Types of Psychotherapy

Okay, but what about when we use treatments that are more difficult to disguise? For example, how could we reduce demand effects if comparing two types of psychotherapy, say cognitive therapy versus behavior therapy, for treating depression? We would be risking demand effects if we were to use one psychotherapist, especially if he or she believed that one of the two types of psychotherapy was more effective. Even though the therapist might try very hard, it would be very difficult not to influence participants.

First, we would need to use more than one therapist. Second, we would need to ask our therapists which treatment type they think is most effective.

Previous research (e.g., Norton, Allen, & Walker, 1985) has shown that people often have very strong beliefs about the comparative effectiveness and desirability of various forms of therapy. One way of reducing bias would be to select therapists who believe that behavior therapy is most effective to deliver the behavior therapy. We would also select those who believe cognitive therapy is most effective to deliver the cognitive therapy. By doing this we would be using only committed therapists.

If we randomly assigned those who believed in behavior therapy and those who believed in cognitive therapy to receive training in both therapy techniques, the "nonbelievers" may not provide therapy as effectively as the believers. Well, you might ask, "What difference would that make? Wouldn't it even out in the end, with both groups of therapists having an equal number of 'believers' and 'nonbelievers'?" True, but this might dilute the effectiveness of both forms of therapy and make it difficult to show that one was more effective than the other.

An alternative approach would be to assign therapists randomly (regardless of beliefs) to the treatment groups and train them using highly specific treatment manuals. These manuals would provide very specific rules on what should be done, and how it should be done, during each session. After training, the therapists could be checked periodically to make sure they were continuing to follow the prescribed protocol. This could be done by videotaping or audiotaping sessions and having them evaluated for compliance with protocol by experienced cognitive and behavior therapists. This type of "manualized" training has been shown to be successful in several studies comparing the effectiveness of treatment programs (e.g., Barlow, 1996). By ensuring that the therapists have followed the appropriate protocol, we can reduce the likelihood of demand effects (and, in cases where a therapist doesn't follow the protocol, data can be eliminated from the study).

More on Using Placebos: Wait-List and Attention Control

When developing a new form of psychotherapy, many clinical researchers will recruit participants who have the disorder they are interested in treating and will randomly assign them to either the treatment group or a "wait-list" group. The wait-list participants may be evaluated at the same points in time as the members of the treatment group, but they do not receive therapy. The results of the study may show that the participants in the treatment group improve more than do those in the wait-list control group. But, these results can't say why they improved more. The differences may simply be due to the amount of attention the treatment group received compared to that of the wait-list group. Indeed, there have been numerous studies showing that people may improve simply because they are in treatment! Being in treatment can, therefore, be a form of an experimenter demand effect—"If I am in treatment, then I should get better."

So, what can we do? One approach would be to show the treatment is more effective than a "credible" placebo (or inactive) treatment or another established treatment. This can be tricky. When comparing an active medication to a placebo, it is relatively easy to create a credible placebo—you put an inactive substance, like sugar, in a capsule and, if desired, add a small amount of another benign substance, such as quinine, to alter the taste. But how can you create a convincing psychotherapy placebo?

You do it in the same way as in a medication study. Simply put, you have to "dress up" the placebo to make it look real or, in other words, make it seem as if it would be effective. This can be done by creating a credible rationale for the placebo treatment by using treatment components that are nonspecific but credible (e.g., letting the participant talk about his or her problems, using relaxation training, or both). Many novels, movies, and other media have used "talk therapy" as an example of effective therapy. This enhances its credibility. Similarly, relaxation therapy has been used as a component of many therapies and is reasonably well known as a nonspecific aid in reducing many types of problems.

When we combine credible components with an effective rationale, we can often create a convincing placebo treatment. This doesn't guarantee that our placebo treatment will be ineffective. It might very well be—simply being in a treatment study can produce powerful changes in a person. However, if these changes were similar in nature and magnitude to our active therapy, we wouldn't have a very powerful therapy for our problem.

It is, unfortunately, often not enough to design a credible placebo. We also have to demonstrate that it is perceived as being as credible as our active treatment. This can be accomplished by asking participants to provide evaluations of the placebo *and* the active treatment prior to their application. To illustrate, after participants have read the treatment rationale (either active or placebo), we might ask them to indicate how effective they think the treatment will be for them. If participants in the placebo group rate the likelihood of their treatment as being as effective as that in the active treatment group, then you know you have a credible placebo treatment.

We might also do periodic evaluations of perceived effectiveness in each group. Even though both groups of participants may have rated their treatments as equally effective prior to application, this may change as the study progresses. If a participant does not see real progress, she may change her mind about the effectiveness of the treatment, regardless of whether she is in the active treatment group or the placebo group. This, in

Illustration 8.2.   Important Factors to Remember About Reducing Experimenter and Participant Demand Characteristics

---

1. Rather than forming specific hypotheses, try to ask questions of nature. This may reduce expectations of what the final results should look like and, as a result, reduce possible demand effects.

2. Try to reduce information that could bias you, as the researcher. Use others, who will not be involved with the participants, to make decisions as to group assignment, type of treatment they receive, and so forth. This will reduce the chances of you unintentionally biasing the data.

3. Work on a need-to-know basis. If possible, don't provide participants with information regarding the experimental or treatment condition they are in or other information that might influence the way they respond in the study. This can be difficult because of ethical issues (see Chapter 6); but, the less information a participant has, the less likely it is that he or she will experience demands to respond in specific ways.

---

turn, could have an effect on how much she improves and, ultimately, on the data being collected.

Summary

Experimenter biases are difficult to prevent, but, as a general rule of thumb, the more committed we are to obtaining a specific result, the more likely we are to cause subtle demand effects. Murray Sidman (1960), in his outstanding book *Tactics of Scientific Research,* maintains that some of our problems with demand effects can be reduced if we simply ask questions of nature rather than form specific hypotheses. When we create hypotheses, we are specifying specific outcomes. According to Sidman, by asking a question of nature using the form, "I wonder what will happen if I ...," we are less likely to expect specific outcomes, and, as a result are less likely to bias our data unwittingly. In clinical research, however, this approach is often not feasible, so we must tailor our research methods in a way that minimizes experimenter bias. Some important points to remember when thinking about reducing experimenter and participant demand effects are provided in Illustration 8.2.

Participant Biases

There are two main classes of participant bias. The first bias is due to differences in the groups that are being evaluated. The second is due to participant attrition over time. Let's use several examples to illustrate each type of participant bias and the similarities and differences between them.

Group Effects

We use a fictional example to describe biases due to differences between groups. Although fictional, the example is based loosely on two studies that were actually reviewed for publication. The studies were not published because the reviewers and, ultimately, the editors of the journals to which the articles had been submitted felt that the data were fatally flawed because of obvious participant biases.

Imagine that two school psychologists working in a large urban school district decided to set up and evaluate a treatment program for children with severe behavior problems. They decided to use only boys for two reasons. First, boys are more likely than girls to exhibit severe behavior problems. Second, they reasoned that combining boys and girls might increase variability because of the different types of behavior problems that each might exhibit. They also decided to restrict their participants to boys in the third grade (again, to reduce variability due to the possibility that boys in different grades may exhibit different behavior problems) who had two parents living at home.

The researchers carefully defined behavior problems as fighting in school and physically or verbally abusing teachers. To qualify for the study, a child had to have engaged in one of the target behaviors on at least two occasions in the past month. So far, so good. The researchers, to this point, have eliminated participant biases due to gender, age, number of parents, and type of behavior problem exhibited by the children—all are the same.

They recruited their participants by sending each third-grade teacher in the school division a letter outlining their study. The teachers were asked to nominate up to three boys in their class who met the criteria for inclusion in the study. The researchers then contacted the parents of the nominated children by letter and then by phone to describe the purpose of the study and to ask if the parents would be interested in enrolling their child in the treatment program. The parents were also asked if they would be willing to participate. Not surprisingly, only about half of the parents agreed to participate along with their children. Another 25% agreed to let their child participate, but declined to participate themselves (citing reasons such as work involvement, lack of time, and so forth, for not participating).

The research design was to include three groups of participants: (a) boys who participated in the treatment program without parental involvement, (b) boys who participated with minimal parental involvement, and (c) those who participated with extensive parental involvement. The noninvolved parents would neither attend therapy sessions with their children, nor would they receive any information about what went on during their child's weekly therapy session. The minimally involved parents would not attend therapy sessions but would receive information after every therapy session along with instructions to use the therapy components with their children throughout the coming week. Finally, the intensively involved parents would attend all sessions with their children and be active participants in the therapy program.

This type of study is technically called a *disentanglement study*. That is, the school psychologists were trying to determine if parental involvement in their children's therapy (and how much of it) was necessary to reduce the boys' behavior problems. If parental involvement was important, the boys with a lot of parental involvement should show better treatment gains than those with minimal involvement who, in turn, should show better gains than those with no parental involvement. To this point, it is a very well designed study. The researchers have eliminated many potential participant biases and have used a study design that will produce important data about the role of parental involvement in treating third-grade boys who have specific types of behavior problems.

The investigators had planned to assign 30 boys and their parents randomly to the three treatment groups. They had chosen 30 for each group based on a careful analysis of how many participants should be in each group to obtain maximum confidence in their findings. Unfortunately, after they obtained parental permission to participate, only 70 child/parent groups and another 30 child/no-parent groups were obtained. As a result, the researchers randomly assigned 30 boys to the intensive parental involvement group, 30 to the minimal parental involvement group, and 10 to the no parental involvement group. They made up the additional 20 members of the no parental involvement group by randomly choosing 20 boys from those whose parents had declined involvement (as this group of children would not have parental involvement during therapy anyway).

After 15 weeks of therapy, the researchers collected data from the schools on how frequently the boys had engaged in fighting and abuse directed toward the teachers during that time. The teachers had all been given reliable and valid checklists that they completed for each boy. The results were consistent with the hypothesis that the greater the parental involvement, the fewer behavior problems noted by the teachers.

See if you can identify the participant bias committed by the researchers that made their data of little value. What is the problem? If you identified the fact that 20 of the participants whose parents had stated they would not be involved in therapy were assigned to the no parental involvement group, you are correct. But, why is this a problem? We can be reasonably confident that intensive parental involvement is more important than minimal involvement. We can't, on the other hand, be confident that parental noninvolvement in treatment was the reason that the no parental involvement group did more poorly than the other two groups. Why? Because we can't be sure that those parents who were unwilling to participate are the same as those who were willing to participate. Even though these parents stated that their unwillingness to participate was due to work and other factors, we can't be certain that they are not generally less involved in their children's lives. So the boys' poor performance may not have been exclusively due to the parents' noninvolvement in therapy, but also due to other factors such as general neglect. This subtle difference between groups completely compromised the soundness of the data.

Attrition Effects

Attrition effects are similar to group effects. In fact, we can think of attrition effects as a subset of group effects. With group effects we get participant biases because the members of different groups differ in some manner that reduces our confidence that any observed outcome differences are the result of our manipulation. Attrition effects occur when participants drop out of a study.

For example, imagine that a research organization had been asked to test a new acne cream, Zitsbegone. The researchers were asked to compare its effectiveness in reducing pimples against an established cream used by a competing company. They advertised for people between the ages of 15 and 20 years and required parental permission from those under 18 years (and a note from their doctor confirming that they had problems with pimples rather than some other skin disorder). One hundred participants were selected and, using a stratified random sampling procedure, two groups were formed, one receiving the new cream and the other the old, established cream. Both groups had an equal number of participants within each age group and an equal number of males and females. The researchers and participants did not know which group was receiving which cream (i.e., they were kept blind). Participants were then individually invited to a briefing on how to use the cream and were given a packet of daily forms to complete and return on a weekly basis during the study. The forms asked a series of questions about the effectiveness of the cream and any possible side effects that might be caused by it.

This went well for the first 2 weeks. Then some of the participants stopped sending in their forms. When these people were phoned and asked to send their forms, most said they were not interested in continuing the study. After the 10 weeks of study, the blind was broken and the researchers were told who was in which group. They found that more than 75% of the 30 dropouts were in the group using Zitsbegone. When they compared the effectiveness of the creams and number of reported side effects, it was found that there were no real differences. Can they conclude that the two creams were equally effective and safe? Based on the information we have provided you, if you say "no," you are correct, but why?

This study presents a classic example of attrition effects. The reason we can't be confident that the two creams were equally effective and safe is that the Zitsbegone group had more than twice the number of dropouts compared to the group using the old, established cream. The greater number of dropouts in the Zitsbegone group may have been due to chance, but it might also have had something to do with differences between the participants in the groups, the creams, or some combination of the two.

Different attrition (drop-out) rates among groups presents a problem for interpreting data and the conclusions we can draw from the results. To accommodate these problems we might try to discover why more people in the Zitsbegone group dropped out. We could, for example, call them and ask why they dropped out. It could be that the dropouts in the Zitsbegone group found that, although the cream seemed to work for the first few weeks, it lost its effectiveness and, as a result, they lost interest in the study. With this information in hand, we might conclude that the two creams, over time, were not equally effective. However, it is sometimes difficult to obtain information from people who have dropped out of a study. We recommend, instead, that you try to obtain as much data about participants as possible before the study starts. Then, at the end of the study these data can be used to compare the characteristics of those who drop out with those who remain in the study.

Sometimes we can find obvious differences between dropouts and those who remain. If so, we can use this information in forming our conclusions about the results of the study. For example, we might have found in our hypothetical study that the dropouts were primarily people who had light complexions. This might lead us to conclude that the two products were equally effective for people with dark complexions, but not for those with light complexions. Without the information about participants, obtained either prior to the onset of the study or after they dropped out, we can only guess as to whether the data based on those who complete the study are representative of the population being studied.

Illustration 8.3.   Important Factors to Remember About Participant Biases

1. If participants' age and sex are expected to produce different patterns of results, either use one age or sex group, or make sure that age and sex are equally distributed across study groups. The technique of equally distributing people who differ in one or more characteristics is called stratified random sampling.

2. Collect data on how credible your experimental conditions are to your participants. If, for example, your placebo or one of your comparison conditions is not as credible as your experimental condition, this could reduce expectations of change or improvement among participants. This information may be useful in showing that participants who drop out are either the same or different from those remaining. This will help with your data analysis and conclusions.

3. Contact those who drop out of your study to try to determine reasons for their discontinuation. It is possible that those who drop out may differ from those who remain in some significant ways.

Summary

Participant biases occur when participants in different groups differ in some important ways. This could be due to group assignment or to factors that are less obvious. Usually we can reduce participant biases by carefully defining our participant population and by using simple randomization procedures when assigning participants to groups. Nevertheless, a researcher must always be careful to ensure that all participant factors are as equal as possible, both at the beginning and at the end of the study. Important factors to remember about participant biases are presented in Illustration 8.3.

Selecting an Appropriate Method

The importance of your method of data collection can't be stressed enough. Indeed, the method dictates how you will go about getting information from your participants. This is apparent in some of the examples used above. Some methods are straightforward and hold relatively few technical challenges. Surveys (whether mail-out, telephone, in-person, retrospective, or prospective) are a good example. Other methods vary considerably in complexity. Indeed, quasi-experimental and experimental methods can be quite simple or exceedingly complex. As we mentioned in Chapter 6, there is really no limit, other than one's imagination, to the variations possible within these general methodologies. The important point to remember here is that your method, which encapsulates your measures, procedures that introduce or control bias, and a number of other factors, has a direct bearing on the soundness of your data. For a more detailed discussion of research methods in clinical psychology we recommend the *Handbook of Research Methods in Clinical Psychology* (Kendall, Butcher, & Holmbeck, 1999).

General Conclusions

The care you take in collecting data will determine the quality of your results. You need to make sure that measures are reliable and valid, make every practical effort to reduce experimental biases, and carefully select the research method that best fits with the question or hypothesis being posed. The guidelines presented in this chapter are meant to provide practical advice that will help you collect the best data possible.

Experimenter and participant biases are very common, and we are often unaware of them. Both can have such powerful influences on our data as to lead to incorrect interpretations of the actual state of affairs. We can never ensure with 100% certainty that we have not permitted experimental biases to affect our data. The best we can do is to be aware of the potential of such effects and to do all that we reasonably can to prevent their occurrence. Even then, we, and others, should always have an interest in replicating research findings. If several independent researchers attempt to replicate findings and all show similar results, we can have much greater certainty in their soundness.

References

Barlow, D. H. (1996). The effectiveness of psychotherapy: Science and policy. *Clinical Psychology: Science and Practice, 3,* 236–240.

Kendall, P. C., Butcher, J. N., & Holmbeck, G. N. (Eds.). (1999). *Handbook of research methods in clinical psychology* (2nd ed.). New York: John Wiley.

Langer, P., & Norton, R. (1965). Structured-objective Rorschach test: A question of choice location. *Perceptual and Motor Skills, 21,* 703–706.

Norton, G. R., Allen, G. E., & Walker, J. R. (1985). Predicting treatment preferences for agoraphobia. *Behavior Research and Therapy, 23,* 699–701.

Sidman, M. (1960). *Tactics of scientific research.* New York: Basic Books.

9

Understanding Variables

When we have lectured or taught courses on research methodology, one of the topics that has been most confusing to our students is that of variables. And with good reason! The term *variable* is used in so many different ways when talking about research methodology. For example, one way the term is used is to indicate that things exist in more than one state— male or female, yes or no, smooth or crunchy peanut butter, and so on. A second way in which the term is used is to describe the things that effect or are effected by what is done in a study. For example, we refer to the *dependent variable* when talking about the measure we use to assess the effect of the *independent variable* or, in other words, what is done to our research participants. See, we told you it could be confusing.

We hope, using our experience, that we can help minimize or prevent this confusion by describing the various ways in which the concept of *variable* is used. If we succeed, at the end of this chapter you will be able to say to others and mean it, "Variables? Of course they are easy to understand. Let me explain them to you."

In this chapter we describe the various ways in which the term variable is used, and through examples, clarify some of the misconceptions of what the different concepts associated with it mean. A second purpose of this chapter is to help you understand when and how each of the different types of variables should be used within the research context.

Variables as Different States

In nature most things exist in more than one state or condition. Some things in nature may normally exist in only dichotomous states. Sex in mammals would be an example—male or female. Other things exist in an almost infinite number of states. A good example of this would be temperature. Temperature can exist, at least theoretically, from absolute zero to billions of degrees above absolute zero. We can even express temperature in fractions of a degree.

Okay, this is the first way in which we use the term variable in research methodology. Things vary in how many units there are of each. We can think of this use of the term as simply a way of mathematically classifying things in nature. Let's take a closer look.

Mathematical Classification

There are two ways in which we can refer to mathematically classified things. First, as we indicated above, some things, such as temperature, can, at least in theory, exist within an infinite series of values. We refer to these as *continuous variables*. With continuous variables, we can even divide a unit into fractions of a unit. Just think of a child who says he is "not five years old," but "five-and-a-fourth years old." Time, and its measure of years, is a continuous variable.

A clinical example of a continuous variable is a score on a questionnaire, such as the Beck Depression Inventory (Beck, Ward, Mendelson, Mock, & Erbaugh, 1961). The Beck Depression Inventory has 21 items, each of which provides the person taking the test with four response options. The first option is selected when symptoms, such as feeling sad or having thoughts of killing oneself, do not apply at all to the respondent. This would be scored as zero. The next three response options indicate increasing severity of the symptom. A person who endorses the first response option on all items would have a total raw score of zero. However, if the person endorsed the response options indicating the greatest symptom severity on all items, he or she would receive a total raw score of 63. Thus, scores on the Beck Depression Inventory represent a continuum of severity of depressive symptoms, ranging from zero to 63.

The second term we wish to introduce related to mathematical classification is *discrete variable* (sometimes also referred to as a categorical variable). Discrete variables can exist in only a finite or limited number of states. Number of children in a family would be an example of a discrete variable. There can be one, two, three, or more children in a family, but partial values (e.g., 1/2) can't exist. Sex is another example. You can be only a male or a female. It is anatomically impossible to be seven-tenths female and three-tenths male (at least, without some type of surgical intervention).

Do you see the difference? Continuous variables can be thought of as being like a string. You can cut the string at an infinite number of places and each length could be slightly longer or shorter than any other length. Discrete variables can be thought of as categorical. Each category can have only one value. Discrete variables can be described only in whole numbers or by category names—one child, two children or male, female.

To complicate the issue, we can (and sometimes want to) convert a continuous variable into a discrete variable. Let's look at an example using the Beck Depression Inventory. Clinically, we might not be interested in a person's raw score (the continuous variable) on the Beck Depression Inventory. We may be interested only in whether the person meets a cut-off score for being depressed versus not depressed. Although such cut-off scores are somewhat arbitrary, Beck et al. (1961) have reported that persons with scores below 11 are not considered to be clinically depressed. Thus, the cut-off scores give us two categories—depressed and not depressed—and, in essence, converts a continuous variable into a discrete one.

Measurement Classification

A second way in which we use the term variable in research methodology is to describe different classifications of measurement. This concept, in and of itself, can be confusing. Try to keep in mind that there are different measurement systems, some of which provide information about nothing more than quality and some that indicate different aspects of quantity. Let's take a look at nominal, ordinal, interval, and ratio variables.

Nominal Variables. Nominal variables express nothing more than differences in quality. They do not provide quantitative information. Sex, racial status, and hair color are examples of nominal variables. Although, for classification purposes, we can assign nominal variables numbers (e.g., Male = 1, Female = 2), these numbers do not convey any quantitative information. By that, we mean that females are not twice whatever males are. Nominal variables, and the numbers we assign them, are used merely for identification. For example, student identification numbers tell us only who the student is; they do not provide any quantitative information on, say, what his or her grade point average is or how many scholarships he or she has been awarded.

In Chapter 2, we described a study done by a group of students who were interested in whether clinical/applied psychologists differed in their interests and activities from those who were primarily interested in experimental psychology. Our classification of psychologists into clinical/applied psychologists and experimental psychologists was an example of creating a nominal variable. Classifying psychologists into the two groups told us only that they differed qualitatively in the type of psychology journals in which they published. Their classification did not provide us with quantitative information on, for example, the number of years each person had been a psychologist, or the number of papers each had published.

Ordinal Variables. Ordinal variables differ in quantity but do not provide information as to the degree to which things differ. To illustrate, let's consider a study where we had members of the Anxiety Disorders Association of America nominate people whom they felt had contributed most to our understanding of anxiety and its disorders (Norton, Asmundson, Cox, & Norton, 2000). We collected nominations via mail (or e-mail, in some cases) and then tabulated the number of nominations each person received. We found that eight people had far more nominations than any of the others. The number of nominations each person received is an example of an ordinal variable. The number of nominations allowed us to rank the leading anxiety researchers; however, this did not provide us with information as to how much greater the contributions made by each over the others were. Ordinal variables can be thought of as *ranking* variables where the absolute, quantitative difference between ranks is unknown.

Another example might be useful for understanding ordinal variables. Let's imagine that four of us have a foot race over 100 meters and that we arrive at the finish line at different times. The first person runs the 100 meters in 12.5 seconds, the second in 13.0 seconds, the third in 18.6 seconds, and the last person in 33.4 seconds. Ordinally, the four runners would come in first, second, third, and fourth. However, the time between arriving at the finish line for the second and first place runners was only 0.5 seconds. The time between the third and second place finishers was 5.6 seconds. Finally, the difference in time for the fourth and third place finishers was 14.8 seconds. The ordinal variable of where each one finished told us nothing about the absolute amount of time it took each runner to finish the race.

Interval Variables. Interval variables have values where the intervals between them are equal. Our two most common measures of temperature—Fahrenheit and Celsius—are good examples of interval variables. Although each uses different numbers to represent the temperature at which water freezes and boils at sea level, both have a consistency to them. For each scale, the difference between 10 and 20 degrees is the same as the difference between 40 and 50 degrees—10 degrees. Fahrenheit and Celsius, even though having equal distances between units (degrees), do not have a true measure of zero degrees. With both scales, we can have temperatures below zero. This means that the unit of zero for interval variables is arbitrary.

The problem with interval variables, where we don't have a true zero, is that we can't make absolute quantitative comparisons. Using temperatures again, we cannot say 40 degrees Celsius is twice as hot as 20 degrees Celsius. However, we could make this kind of comparison if we use a scale, or variable, that has an absolute zero (e.g., a person who is 2 meters tall is twice the height of a person who is 1 meter).

Many of the most common measures in social and medical sciences are interval variables and, as a result of not having a true zero, we are prevented from making true quantitative comparisons between two values of the measure. For example, measures of intelligence, or IQ, are based on interval variables. As a result, we can't state that a person with an IQ of 150 is twice as intelligent as one with an IQ of 75.

Ratio Variables. Ratio variables are like interval variables in that there is equal spacing between units. They differ from interval variables in that they have a true zero. Ratio variables permit us to make quantitative comparisons in terms of absolute values. For example, with ratio variables such as height and weight, we can determine that a person who weighs 80 kilograms is twice as heavy as one who weighs 40 kilograms. We also have a ratio scale for temperature—the Kelvin scale. Zero on the Kelvin scale represents absolute zero, a point at which there can be no atomic activity (e.g., electron flow). Blood pressure is also an example of a ratio scale. If there is no blood flow, a person would not have a detectable blood pressure (and would likely be dead). The absolute zero allows us to say that a person who has a systolic blood pressure of 200 mg of mercury has a pressure that is exactly twice as high as someone with a systolic blood pressure of 100 mg of mercury. This knowledge would be important to a cardiologist who is testing the effects of new blood pressure medications.

Summary

Illustration 9.1 outlines six important things to remember about measurement variables. Nominal variables provide only information about qualitative differences between groups and do not yield quantitative information. Ordinal, interval, and ratio variables all provide quantitative information, but they differ in the types of information that can be derived.

The description of different types of variables may seem unnecessarily complicated and trivial; but the type of variable determines the type of mathematical operations that we can perform on the data. In Chapter 10 we describe basic statistical operations that permit us to determine if there are, for example, differences between groups that have been given different

Illustration 9.1.   Important Things to Remember About Measurement Variables

---

1. The term variable can be used to describe how many states in which something can exist. Discrete variables can take on only a certain defined number of states. For example, with few exceptions at the chromosomal level, mammals are typically only one of two states of sex, male and female. Continuous variables can exist in an infinite number of states. For example, temperatures can vary from absolute zero to (theoretically) millions of degrees.

2. Variables can be used to express qualitative and quantitative differences between things. Nominal variables provide only qualitative information about items. They "name" things.

3. Variables that provide quantitative information differ in the type of information they convey. Ordinal variables convey only information about rank order. They do not provide information about the number of units that separate different ranks.

4. Interval and ratio variables both have values with equal intervals between them. However, because interval variables have arbitrary zero points, they cannot express true multiples. That is, on an interval scale a value of 20 does not represent twice as much as 10.

5. The values of ratio variables, which have true zero points, can express true multiples.

6. The different types of variables require different types of statistics for their evaluation.

---

treatments. In this case, we can't make these types of comparisons between measures that are based on nominal variables. In order to perform these statistical operations we must ensure that we have the appropriate variable types. A critical point to remember is that some types of statistical analyses are inappropriate to use with some types of variables and, if applied in this way, can lead to meaningless results and conclusions.

Experimental Classification

For purposes of research, we can manipulate or vary variables, we can measure them, or they can affect our results in unplanned ways unless we control for them. We have terms for each of these actions. They are independent,

Illustration 9.2.   Basic Features of Independent, Dependent, and Extraneous Variables

Variable Type	Main Feature
Independent	The condition or feature that is manipulated or varied to produce changes in the participant's performance
Dependent	The data that are collected when doing research
Extraneous	Nuisances that affect the outcome of data collection in an unplanned or uncontrolled way

dependent, and extraneous variables. Let's look at each in detail. You can refer to Illustration 9.2 for an overview of the general differences between these types of variables.

Independent Variables

The independent variable of a research study refers to the condition that is manipulated or varied to produce changes in our participant's performance. In the hypothetical study we described in Chapter 8, where a researcher was comparing a new acne cream against one that was already on the market, the type of acne cream used was the independent variable. The independent variable is under the control of the researcher. That is, the researcher assigns the type of acne cream to the participants *independent* of their particular type of skin condition or their type of acne. The participants were given each type of cream on a randomized basis.

There are a several types of independent variables. Following the lead of Kazdin (1992), we define three types—environmental or situational, instructional, and participant variables. These are summarized in Illustration 9.3.

Environmental or Situational Variables. With environmental or situational variables, the researcher alters the environment or situation of a study. That is, the researcher changes or manipulates "what is done to, with, or by the subject" (Kazdin, 1992). The study of acne creams is an example of the use of an environmental or situational variable. In this study, the researcher varied the type of cream used by different participants. By doing so, the environment of different participants was altered.

When using environmental or situational independent variables the researcher can provide

Illustration 9.3.   Types of Independent Variables

1. Environmental or situational variables: The researcher manipulates the study by way of altering participant condition/task or quality/quantity of treatment.

2. Instructional variables: The researcher manipulates information provided to participants in order to influence and observe their thoughts, feelings, or actions.

3. Participant variables: Participant characteristics that cannot be manipulated are selected by the researcher on the basis of different features.

---

1. a condition or task to some participants, but not to others (treatment vs. no treatment);

2. different amounts of a treatment to different groups of participants (different level of treatment); or

3. qualitatively different conditions to different groups of participants (different treatments).

Let's look at examples of each of the above scenarios. There are two basic forms of manipulating the independent variable in the treatment/no-treatment condition. In the first, classic scenario, some participants receive treatment and others don't. In the second, some participants receive treatment and others are put on a wait-list. The primary difference between the two approaches is that it is expected that the participants in the wait-list group will, eventually, receive the same treatment as those in the treatment group.

These are the weakest approaches to evaluating the effects of an independent variable. With either of the treatment/no-treatment approaches, we can't be sure that the changes in outcome between the treatment and no-treatment groups are due to our experimental manipulation or, instead, to other factors extraneous to our study. For example, it may be that the participants in the treatment group showed greater change than did those in the no-treatment group simply because they were receiving attention from the researchers and those in the no-treatment group were not. The difference in level of attention, and not our treatment, may be responsible for some or all observed changes.

A third, stronger approach is to assign participants randomly to groups that receive different levels of the independent variable. We refer to this as the different levels of treatment approach. For example, let's suppose that the researcher who was evaluating the new acne cream had found that the cream was, indeed, better that the conventionally used cream. Now, the researcher might want to determine if different concentrations of the cream had any effect on the number of blemishes people had after using the cream. One strategy might be to assign some participants to zero effective ingredients (placebo), others to 5 units, and yet others to 10 units. In all three conditions, the tubes of cream would look the same so as to minimize obvious differences in treatment conditions. This manipulation of the independent variable would allow the researcher to determine if some treatment (5 or 10 units) was better than no treatment, and if one level of treatment was superior to the other. This is a very sophisticated way in which to manipulate an independent variable.

Finally, qualitative manipulation of the independent variable can involve the use of two or more qualitatively different treatments. Our original example of comparing two different acne creams, as opposed to different levels of active ingredient in the same cream, is an example. Another example would be testing the effects of Paxil alone versus Paxil plus cognitive behavior therapy in the treatment of Panic Disorder; assuming the same dose of Paxil is used in each condition, these two treatment approaches are qualitatively different.

Instructional Variables.   Instructional variables refer to those where participants in different groups are provided different information. The purpose of manipulating instructional variables is to determine if different types of information provided orally, in written form, or otherwise, influence behavior or cognition. A well-known study, supposedly on the effects of noise on routine performance, is an excellent example of how researchers manipulated instructional variables.

Glass and Singer (1972) randomly assigned participants to two groups. Both groups were exposed to a loud noise while performing a routine task such as crossing out all of the *e* letters on a page of text. One group was told that if the noise became too bothersome, they could push a button that was situated near them. The other group was not provided information about the button. In fact, the button was not hooked up, and had no control over the noise level. Interestingly, none of the participants in either group actually used the button. The results of the study showed that the group that was led to believe (via instructions) that they could control the noise level performed the task much more efficiently than did those who had not been instructed that they could control the noise.

Let's look at another example. Schachter (1959), in a clever study, manipulated information that participants received through tone of voice, appearance, and actual content. The participants, all young female university students, were asked to participate in a study involving learning new information. After the participants arrived at the laboratory, they were told that the study involved electric shock. However, the information about the shock and the manner in which it was delivered varied dramatically. The students were randomly assigned to one of two conditions. In the first, the researcher was dressed casually, had a pleasant manner, and told the participants that the shock was mild and that they would barely feel it. In the second, the participants were greeted by a stern looking individual who wore a lab coat, had a brusque manner, and told the participants that the shock would be quite severe. After receiving information about the shock, which was never actually delivered, the participants were told that there would be a brief delay while the laboratory was being set up. Each participant was then asked if she would prefer to wait alone or with others while waiting her turn to participate.

The dependent variable, or the measure of interest, which is discussed in the next section of this chapter, was whether the participant chose to be alone or with others while waiting her turn. The results were very interesting. The women who believed that they were going to receive strong shocks were much more likely to choose to be with others than those who believed that the shock would be mild.

In short, instructional variables include manipulating or varying information that lead participants to have different beliefs or attitudes, or to behave differently. Instructional variables can be manipulated by telling participants different things, providing them with different written information, having them observe different things, or combinations of all the above.

Participant Variables. These variables refer to characteristics or features of the participants. They are not manipulated. Rather, participants for a study are selected because of having different features. Participant (or individual difference) variables include such things as age, gender, social class, and personality characteristics.

An example of the use of a participant variable is our recent study (Norton et al., 1996) comparing people who had Panic Disorder with those who had Social Phobia. In this study we compared the two groups on a number of dependent variables such as education, marital status, and several aspects of mental health. The diagnosis—Panic Disorder versus Social Phobia—was our independent variable. Likewise, Sulloway (1997), a historian, in his wonderful book *Born to Rebel,* used birth order, another example of a participant variable, as his independent variable. He compared first born, middle born, and later born people on creativity, finding that most of the revolutionary ideas in art, science, and politics came from later born children.

Participant variables are especially useful to clinical researchers. Many of the questions asked by clinical researchers involve dimensions of differences between participants. A medical researcher might be interested in determining whether people diagnosed with cancer have higher suicide rates than those without cancer. Similarly, a psychologist studying pain behaviors might be interested in determining whether people with similar injuries who score high versus low on a measure of "fear of pain" take more pain medication and are more likely to be disabled.

To summarize, participant variables are based on differences among various groups we are interested in. They can include age, gender, personality, and so on. The critical feature of a participant variable is that participants in one group are selected on the basis of a personal characteristic that differs from that of the members of other groups.

Dependent Variables

You already know what dependent variables are. We have mentioned them above and discussed them in detail in Chapter 7 (but didn't refer to them using this term). They are the data that are collected when doing research. The term *dependent variable* refers to the idea that these variables are, to a degree, dependent on the manipulations performed on the independent variable. We'll explain what we mean by this. In an earlier chapter we described a study where we gave people with Panic Disorder brief cognitive behavior therapy (Stein, Norton, Walker, Chartier, & Graham, 2000). In addition, one half of the participants received an antidepressant, Paxil, and one half a placebo. Our primary interest was to determine if the addition of Paxil to cognitive behavior therapy decreased the frequency of panic attacks more than the addition of placebo. Our primary dependent variable was frequency of panic attacks. If our manipulation of our independent variable—Paxil versus placebo—produced a difference in number of panic attacks experienced by members of the two groups, then we could say that the number of panic attacks was dependent upon the type of treatment received.

Remember, as discussed in Chapter 7, that a dependent variable can be based on self-reports, behavioral measures, or physiological measures. In addition, keep in mind that most studies include several dependent variables—you need not limit yourself to one. In fact, combining variables across categories is an excellent research strategy. By combining variables you can often gain more information than would be obtained by using a single type of measure. You can also use several different measures within a category. For example, in the study described above, comparing Paxil and placebo, we obtained self-report measures of depression and general anxiety, as well as frequency of panic attacks. By doing this we might have observed other important things, such that people who were more depressed had more panic attacks or that cognitive behavior therapy plus Paxil was more effective than cognitive behavior therapy plus placebo in reducing depression. Note, however, that when using several measures within a category, you should be careful to determine that the information you are gathering does not overlap markedly. If two or more of your measures overlap extensively, you are likely in a situation where you are wasting not only your time, but also that of the participants.

To summarize, dependent variables are those things that we measure to determine if our manipulation of the independent variable produces differences in our participants. Dependent variables for most clinical research will be either self-reports, physiological measures, measures of behavior, or some combination of these.

Extraneous Variables

A better term for extraneous variables would be *nuisance variables*. These are things that can affect the outcome of a study, and they do so in an unplanned and uncontrolled manner. Let's look at a hypothetical example. Imagine that we are interested in the effects of music on a person's ability to solve problems. We randomly assign 120 people to listen to rap music, classical music, and cool jazz while solving a series of puzzles. Because we can accommodate only 30 people at a time in the laboratory, we decide to do our testing over 2 days. On Day 1, we arrange for those who are listening to rap to show up at our laboratory 9:00 a.m., those listening to classical music at 1:00 p.m., and finally those listening to jazz at 4:00 p.m. The next day, we reverse the order so that those listening to jazz are tested first, followed by those listening to classical, and finally those listening to rap.

After we have collected and scored the results of the problem-solving task for the participants tested on Day 1, we find that those who listened to rap music solved significantly more puzzles than did those who listened to jazz. The group that listened to classical music fell midway between the rap and jazz groups. However, when we evaluate the results of the participants tested on Day 2 we get the opposite results. Those who listened to jazz performed best on the problem-solving task. What's up?

What's up is that we were broadsided by a powerful extraneous variable—time of day. For purposes of illustration, we can imagine that the effect of time of day was greater than that of the type of music listened to. Those participants who were tested later in the day were likely more fatigued and, regardless of type of music listened to, their problem-solving skills were diminished. If we run our study on only one day, say Day 1, we would have come to conclusions that were potentially erroneous.

Extraneous variables can be the result of unplanned and uncontrolled participant variables (e.g., personality, age) or environmental variables (e.g., time of day, temperature differences). The key factor is that something that we did not want (or account for) acts to change the outcome of our study in unpredictable ways. Notice that throughout our discussion of extraneous variables we have emphasized the concepts of *unplanned* or *uncontrolled* effects. Well, these concepts suggest how we can reduce the effects of extraneous variables. In reality, we can never totally eliminate extraneous variables simply because we can never know with certainty all those things that can influence our data. What we can do, however, is try to anticipate the extraneous variables that might have the greatest effects on our results and try to eliminate them.

How? Well, we can reduce their effects in several ways. First, we can try to prevent their occurrence. In the example above, we could have tested everyone at the same time of day on the same day in the same room. By doing that, we would have eliminated time of day, day of the week, and characteristics of the room (e.g., temperature, lighting conditions) as variables. These would have been constant for all participants. Because we could accommodate only 30 people at a time this, unfortunately, would be an impossible solution. So, we would need to try alternative solutions. One might be to have some members of each music group tested at the same time. For example, by having the participants wear headphones, they could listen simultaneously to different types of music.

Random assignment is the second, and often the most practical, way of reducing the effects of extraneous variables. If we randomly assign participants to our various conditions (i.e., treatment groups, time of day), we are hoping that extraneous variables have an equal chance of appearing in each of the conditions and, thereby, neutralizing their effects.

Finally, if we cannot prevent or control for the effects of extraneous variables, we can try to control for them statistically. Although this is usually an undesirable method for reducing the effects of extraneous variables, it is sometimes the only way to do so. The statistical procedures, such as Analysis of Covariance, that can be used in this regard are beyond the scope of this book. Most of the higher-level statistics books (e.g., Tabachnick & Fidell, 1996) provide good explanations of these.

To summarize, extraneous variables are things that can affect data in ways that are not planned for. In some cases, the effects of extraneous variables can be more powerful than the effects of an independent variable. Although it is almost impossible to eliminate extraneous variables completely, we need to be aware of the potential effects they may have and try to reduce or eliminate them as best we can.

Summary

The term variable can mean different things. We have described three ways in which the term is used in clinical research. First, variables can describe how many of something exists. Some things can be described in only discrete states, such as male or female. Others can exist on an infinite continuum, such as temperature or distance. We then expanded and refined this concept by describing the way variables are used in measurement classification. One class of variables—nominal variables—is used only to categorize or name variables. Three types of measurement variables provide increasing measurement sophistication. Ordinal variables express rank order but do not provide information about how much the ranks differ in space or time. Interval variables have equal distances between numbers, but, because they have arbitrary zero points, can't denote absolute differences. Ratio variables have equal distances between each number and an absolute zero point. An important point to remember is that statistical procedures appropriate to one class of measurement variables may not be appropriate to another. In fact, this is usually the case.

We also described how the term variable is used in experimental classification. This category of variable usage is the most commonly used in clinical research. Basic details of independent variables (those that the researcher manipulates), dependent variables (those that are measured or, in other words, are dependent on the manipulated variable), and extraneous variables (those nuisance variables that must be eliminated or controlled for) were provided.

Variables are the "stuff" of research. Despite their importance to the research process, they are often misunderstood. We hope this chapter has increased your understanding of the many ways in which variables are used in clinical research. We also hope that you will now be able to explain these uses to others.

References

Beck, A. T., Ward, C. H., Mendelson, M., Mock, J., & Erbaugh, J. (1961). An inventory for measuring depression. *Archives of General Psychiatry, 4,* 561–571.
Glass, D. C., & Singer, J. E. (1972). *Urban stress: Experiments on noise and social stressors.* New York: Academic Press.

Kazdin, A. E. (1992). *Research designs in clinical psychology* (2nd ed.). Needham Heights, MA: Allyn & Bacon.

Norton, G. R., McLeod, J., Guertin, J., Hewitt, P. L., Walker, J. R., & Stein, M. B. (1996). Panic Disorder or Social Phobia: Which is worse. *Behaviour Research and Therapy, 34,* 273–276.

Norton, P. J., Asmundson, G. J. G., Cox, B. J., & Norton, G. R. (2000). Future directions in anxiety disorders: Profiles and perspectives of leading contributors. *Journal of Anxiety Disorders, 14,* 69–95.

Schachter, S. (1959). *The psychology of affiliation.* Stanford, CA: Stanford University Press.

Stein, M. B., Norton, G. R., Walker, J. R., Chartier, M. J., & Graham, R. (2000). Do selective serotonin reuptake inhibitors enhance the efficacy of very brief cognitive behavioral therapy for Panic Disorder? A pilot study. *Psychiatry Research, 94,* 191–200.

Sulloway, F. (1997). *Born to rebel: Birth order, family dynamics, and creative lives.* Mississauga, ON: Random House of Canada.

Tabachnick, B. G., & Fidell, L. S. (1996). *Using multivariate statistics* (3rd ed.). New York: HarperCollins.

10

Handling Data and Using Statistics

I n the previous chapters we highlighted issues that are important to collecting data. Once collected, we need to "look" at the data. By this we mean not only looking at it in the literal sense, such as when checking for errors in a database, but also analyzing it using statistical techniques. How is your statistical savvy? In our experience, statistics can be one of the most difficult areas for clinical researchers. "What does this statistic mean?" "Why was that statistic used?" "Are the findings important to clinical practice?" Such questions arise regardless of whether one has had one or even numerous courses in statistics. The primary purpose of this chapter is to (re)acquaint you with the *basic* concepts of statistics and their use in analyzing data. We look at some of the most common statistical concepts that you are likely to encounter when reading or conducting research—descriptive statistics, probability theory, tests of the significance of differences between grouped data, and correlation-based statistics. Even those of you with more advanced statistical training may find the material to be a good refresher.

Except in a few instances, we do not provide information on how to compute the various statistics we discuss. If you want to learn how they are derived, you may wish to consult textbooks on basic statistical analyses, such as *Statistics for the Behavioral Sciences* (Gravetter & Wallnau, 1999), *Statistical Applications for the Behavioral Sciences* (Grimm, 1993), and *Statistics: A Gentle Introduction* (Coolidge, 2000). For information on the more advanced statistics we recommend *Using Multivariate Statistics* (Tabachnick & Fidell, 1996), as well as many of the books in Sage's Quantitative Applications in the Social Sciences Series (see www.sagepub.com or www. sagepub.co.uk).

It is fair to say that if you don't have a good grasp of statistics, you should, as recommended in Chapter 5, consider recruiting someone who does have the necessary knowledge to assist with the statistical aspects of your research. This may be your mentor or it may be a hired consultant. Someone with knowledge of your area of research will be better able to assist you in designing your study, selecting the appropriate statistics at an early stage (preferably before data collection begins), and analyzing your data.

It is also fair to say that the majority of statistical analyses that you run on your data will be done using a computerized statistical package. So, why spend time on understanding the basics when a computer will do it for you and simply "spit out" the numbers in a matter of milliseconds? Well, the answer relates not only to the knowledge base upon which you make decisions about your own research, but also to a secondary purpose of this chapter. This secondary purpose is to build upon our discussions in Chapter 4 regarding your critical reading skills. Here we hope to provide you with some of the basic information necessary to understand and begin to make critical decisions about the results that are presented in many of the articles you read. By reviewing research articles that are similar to the type of study you are planning, you will gain a wider perspective on issues pertinent to the area as a whole, the need for your study, and, importantly, the types of statistical analyses that can best be applied to your data.

A Word on Creating and Cleaning Electronic Databases

By this point it should be obvious that clinical researchers do a lot to avoid the influences of error. Our sampling procedures are geared toward reducing it as much as possible. We go to great lengths to ensure that the measures we use are reliable and valid. As you will see below, we set allowable levels of probability that our findings are due to chance. There is concern about Type I and Type II errors. Our procedures for critically evaluating the work of others are designed to find value but also to identify potential shortcomings and, if present, error in method, statistics, or interpretation of findings. The bottom line is that we, as clinical researchers, need to avoid error if our contributions are going to be meaningful!

Would you be surprised to hear that your database may contain errors? If you (or a research assistant) have entered data into a computerized database, whether manually or via electronic transfer from an online collection, but have not "cleaned" it, then the chances are pretty good that some errors are present. These errors will, obviously, influence the results of your research in an unpredictable manner that will ultimately mislead your research efforts. So, you need to ensure that your data is error free before analyzing it. How? There are many approaches to cleaning data and, to some degree, they depend on the nature of the data and the manner in which they were collected. You may find the following general guidelines useful.

- If using self-report survey data, researcher/clinician-administered survey data, or data measured or coded directly by the researcher, start by checking that all values fall within the appropriate or expected range. An easy method of doing this is to create a frequency distribution and to scan visually for values beyond the range. For example, if the possible range of scores on items of a survey is 1 through 5, then any other values in the database for this survey would be in error. Another method is to enter the data and then have them re-entered by an assistant with the purpose of watching for errors in the initial entry. We prefer a combination of these two strategies.

- If using data from an online sampling of physiological parameters, or automated measures of responses such as reaction times, it is necessary to check that "noise" or software errors have been removed from the data. This is often done automatically by the software used to collect this type of data. However, some errors do sneak in. As per the suggestion above, you can create frequency distributions and look for unusually high or low scores. In this case, however, the measured variables may not (and likely do not) have predefined ranges. A typical strategy is to remove data points that fall outside of 2 or 3 standard deviations of the mean. We discuss the concept of standard deviation in greater detail below.

- If using surveys, be certain that any reverse-scored items are coded correctly. Assume, for example, that you have an item score range of 1 to 5 on a survey. The score for Item 12 is 2. But, Item 12 is reverse scored. This means that your database should denote the score as 4 (because in reverse-scoring $1 = 5, 2 = 4, 3 = 3, 4 = 2$, and $5 = 1$). Failure to account for reverse-scoring will transform potentially valuable data into misleading garbage.

- If using formulas to calculate total and subscale scores electronically, be certain that the formulas you enter are correct. Check and double-check your formula before running it. A good strategy is to enter and run the formula and then, as a new variable in the database, do the same thing again. If the formula was entered correctly on both attempts, then there should be perfect correspondence between the two calculated scores. You can then delete one of these variables, given that they are identical, and proceed.

- Pay careful attention to the manner in which you handle missing data. Different software programs often use different methods for coding missing data. For example, some use a blank space, some use a decimal point, some use a "9," and some allow you to choose otherwise impossible values, such as "999." Whatever method you use, be certain that you do not mistake missing values for data or vice versa!

- If combining two or more sets of data, be certain that the data from each of the files are configured so that they (a) contain the same participants (you might start by checking that there are an equal number of participants in each set), and (b) are ordered the same (you might start by using a "*sort*" command to arrange each set by participant identification number). This should help ensure that, when combined, the data for a participant from one set correspond with the data for the *same partic-ipant* in the other set. Failure to merge data sets accurately, again, can turn mean-ingful data into misleading garbage.

- Label everything! *Label, in detail, all of the variables in your databases.* Do this elec-tronically in the database, but also keep a detailed paper file of variable names, def-initions, scoring formulas, and so on. Also, label all combined databases, including full and partial (subset) merges, with the purpose (you might use a short study title) and date of the merger. It is not unusual to come back to a database after months or years. Nor is it unusual to share it with a colleague. Imagine trying to recall or explain the specific details of your variables or various database mergers without the aid of labels!

You also need to take care in the technical aspects of creating your data-base. Be certain that the software you use for entering your data is com-patible with the software that will be used to run the statistical analyses. This seems obvious, but we have frequently encountered situations where colleagues have sought our assistance with statistical analysis only to find that it is in a format that is incompatible with our statistical software. In some instances, the solution is simple—the database can be converted into a usable format electronically. This, however, is not always the case and, unfortunately, sometimes the only solution is to re-enter (and re-clean) the data. Augh! The message here is that a little advanced planning regarding the "who and how" of your statistical analyses is an excellent strategy that may pay big dividends in the long run.

Descriptive Statistics

Descriptive statistics are just what the name suggests—they are statistics that organize and describe sets of data. There are two types of descriptive statistics. These are measures of *central tendency* and measures of *variation*. They are the building blocks of inferential statistics, which, as you will see below, allow us to draw inferences (or conclusions) about differences and similarities in sets of data. Before we look at descriptive statistics, we should review the ways in which data are distributed. This information is of particular importance for understanding descriptive statistics and probability estimates, which we discuss in the next section.

Illustration 10.1. Normal Bell-Shaped Curve

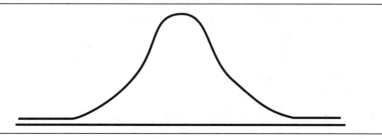

Data Distribution

Most of the phenomena of interest to clinical researchers are distributed in *normal* or bell-shaped curves (see Illustration 10.1). This means that most of the scores cluster in the middle of the distribution and that there are fewer intermediate scores and even fewer low and high scores. For most statistical procedures used in clinical research, it is important that the data obtained are distributed in a normal curve. Sometimes, if we use only small samples or if we don't use randomly selected samples, we can get highly *skewed distributions*. This means that the majority of the scores cluster at either the low or high end of the distribution, rather than in the middle.

An understanding of the concept of a normal curve is of central importance to an understanding of descriptive statistics. Let's consider some hypothetical data. Imagine that we are great fans of Julia Roberts, currently the highest paid female actor in Hollywood. We wonder if her appeal might be due, at least in part, to her very wide smile. Further, when we look at the literature, we find that there are very few data on the widths of smiles for either males or females. (Using your literature searching skills you might check to see if this is really the case.) So, we decide to measure the smile widths of a random sample of females to determine if Ms. Roberts's smile really is unusually wide. We ask our participants to make their widest smile while we measure it using very exacting calipers. After measuring smile widths of 100 women, we notice that, although they only vary by less than 15 millimeters, there is quite a large variation in the size of smiles. Figure 10.1 illustrates our hypothetical data. The numbers on the Y-axis (vertical line) represent the number of females who have smiles of a certain width. The number of cases in each category is referred to as the frequency score. The numbers on the X-axis (horizontal line) represent smile widths, in millimeters.

The figure shows that smile widths varied from 65 mm to 77 mm. However, only 4 of our participants had smiles as small as 65 mm or as wide as 77 mm. The majority of participants had smiles of approximately 71 mm. Our fictional data show that there is almost a step-by-step increase

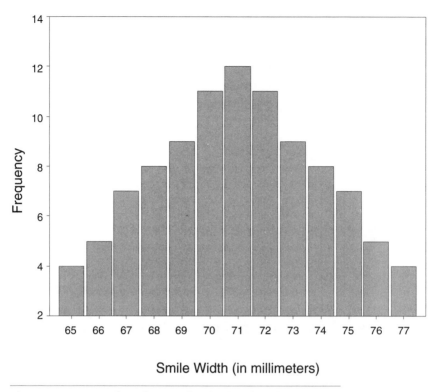

Figure 10.1.   Hypothetical, Normally Distributed Smile Width Data

in frequency of participants with smile widths of 65 mm to 71 mm, and then an equal decline in frequency to 77 mm. Our data are perfectly normal (and, if you want, you could draw a normal curve, like the one in Illustration 10.1, through them).

Now, let's imagine that we are interested in the family incomes of people in the core area of a large city. We randomly select 100 households and interview the owners to determine their total household annual income. Figure 10.2 shows the data collected in our survey, with the number of people earning a particular income on the Y-axis and income levels on the X-axis. The data show that the majority of people with low incomes are bunched up on the left side of the graph with fewer and fewer families making higher incomes. This is an example of skewed data. When data are bunched on the left side (most are low scores), we say that the distribution is *positively skewed*. If most of the scores occur on the right side (high scores), we say the distribution is *negatively skewed*. Skewed data are not normally distributed and, if excessively skewed, they can distort our statistical analyses in an unpredictable manner. We address this issue below in greater detail.

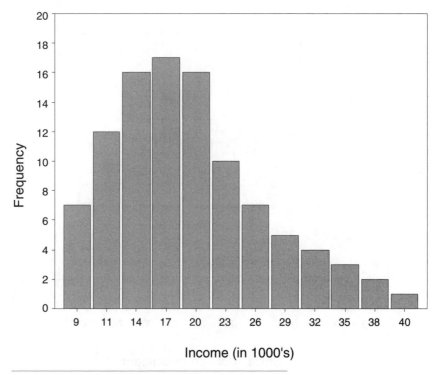

Figure 10.2.   Hypothetical, Skewed Family Income Data

Measures of Central Tendency

The three most commonly used measures of central tendency are the mean, mode, and median. We will use the data in our two hypothetical distributions shown above to look at each of these three measures. The term *mean* is what is usually referred to as the *average* for a distribution of scores. *Mode* refers to the most common score in a distribution. *Median* refers to the middle-most score in the distribution of numbers that are arranged from lowest to highest.

Before we use our two hypothetical sets of data, let's review what is meant by the terms mean, mode, and median using a simple example. Consider the following numbers—1, 2, 3, 4, 5, 5, 6, 7, 8, and 9. To calculate the mean, we must first sum all the scores and divide by the number of scores. This is represented by the formula $\Sigma\, Xi/N = \bar{X}$, where Σ = the sum of individual scores in the distribution, Xi = each individual score, N = the number of scores, and $\bar{X}$ = the mean. When we add all the individual scores we get a total of 50. We have a total of 10 individual scores. Dividing 50 by 10 = 5. Five is our mean or average score. What about the mode? Remember, the mode is the most commonly occurring score. In our sample distribution, all of the scores except 5 occur only one time. The number 5 occurs twice. Because it is our most common score, it is our mode. In some distributions, we can have more than one mode. If two scores occur more than any other, but occur an equal number of times, we have two modes (or a bimodal distribution).

What about the median? When you look at the numbers 1, 2, 3, 4, 5, 5, 6, 7, 8, and 9, you can see that there are four scores smaller than 5 and four scores larger. Thus, the two scores of 5 represent the middle-most score. What if we had only one 5 in our distribution? There would still be four scores smaller than 5 and four scores larger than 5. Thus, 5 would still be our median. Now, what would be the median of this distribution: 1, 2, 3, and 4? There is no one score that represents the exact middle of the distribution. Therefore, because we assume that each score includes all partial scores (i.e., the number 2 represents a set of scores ranging from 2.00 to 2.99), we have to select a value that represents the middle of the distribution. Our median would be midway between 2.00 and 3.00. Thus, in this case, it would be 2.50. Now, to challenge you even more, let's consider this distribution: 1, 2, 5, and 6. What would the median be? To calculate the median when there are missing values, we presume they are there. So, for purposes of calculating the median we change our distribution to look like this: 1, 2, (3, 4), 5, 6. Now, we simply find the middle-most score, which is half way between 3.00 and 4.00. Thus, our median would be 3.50.

Let's calculate the mean, mode, and median of the data presented to in Figures 10.1 and 10.2. Although the methods for calculating the mean, mode, and median are the same for all distributions, computing from a normally distributed data set is much simpler than when using skewed data.

Because we have more than one person with each of our 13 different smile widths, we have set up a frequency table (see Table 10.1) for the data. This allows us to compute the mean more easily. Remember, the formula for the mean is $\Sigma\, Xi\, /\, N$. When we divide our Σ of 7,100 by our N of 100 we obtain a mean of 71.0. Okay, now by examining the data in Figure 10.1 and Table 10.1, we can determine the mode and median. The most commonly occurring score, the mode, is 71. When we count from the lowest scores upward we find there are 44 scores ranging from 65 to 70 centimeters. Working backward, we can see that there are also 44 scores from 77 to 72 centimeters. This leaves 71 centimeters as the middle score in the distribution. Thus, our median is 71.

Table 10.1 Measures of Central Tendency for Hypothetical Normally Distributed Female Smile Width Data

	No. of Cases	Smile Width	Total
	4	65	260
	5	66	330
	7	67	469
	8	68	544
	9	69	621
	11	70	770
	12	71	852
	11	72	792
	9	73	657
	8	74	592
	7	75	525
	5	76	380
	4	77	308
ΣXi	100		7,100
Mean		71	
Mode		71	
Median		71	

Notice that the mean in the above example is the same as the mode and the median. This can occur only when the distribution of scores is perfectly symmetrical. This is very rare! Using the data presented in Table 10.2, let's look at how asymmetry (or skewness) affects our measures of central tendency.

We have to make some assumptions about this distribution. First, we used $9,000 for our first category even though we included those with a family income of less than $9,000. Second, because we were using categories, or ranges of family incomes, we chose the middle-most income from each group. For example, for those who had incomes from $16,000 to $18,000 we chose as our statistic the middle score of $17,000. These assumptions may slightly affect our true measures of central tendency because, for example, there may have been more families with incomes of $16,000 than those making $18,000. This would make our statistic of $17,000 slightly higher than it should be. Ideally, we would compute our measures of central tendency using the original family income scores. However, for convenience sake, we will use the values in Table 10.2 for illustrative purposes.

Let's start by computing our mean. When we total our scores we find that we have a total of 1,934. We also have 100 participants. Thus when we divide our N into our ΣXi, we get a mean family income of 19.34 or $19,340. Figure 10.2 and Table 10.2 show that 17 families had incomes of $17,000. More families had this income than any other. Thus our mode is 17 or $17,000. When we count the number of families from the lowest

Table 10.2   Measures of Central Tendency for Hypothetical Family Income Data

Number of Cases	Family Annual Income (in $000s)	Total (in $000s)
7	<9	63
12	11	132
16	14	224
17	17	289
16	20	320
10	23	230
7	26	182
5	29	145
4	32	145
3	35	105
2	38	76
1	>40	40
Σ Xi	100		1,934
Mean		19.34	
Mode		17.00	
Median		16.76	

income up, we find that 52 families have incomes of $17,000 or less. Because we need the middle-most number of 50, we need to do some more calculations. Remember that the family income of $17,000 actually represents the category of families earning from $16,000 to $18,000. Let's assume that families had incomes ranging in equal steps from $16,000 to $18,000. If we divide the 17 families into $2,000, the range of salaries in this category, we find that there are increments of $117.64 between family incomes. The lowest-earning family in the category made $16,000, the next $16,117.64, and so on, to the maximum of $18,000. Because there were 52 families with incomes of $17,000 or less, we need to take two family increments away from $17,000 to obtain the true median family income. Each increment was $117.64, so two would be $235.28. When we subtract this from $17,000 we find that the true family median income was $16,764.72.

Why are we so concerned with each of these measures of central tendency? The simple answer is that they help summarize a distribution of scores. Measures of central tendency give us various simple statistics that help us describe our data. However, some measures of central tendency are better than others. The mode, for example, provides us with little information except to tell us which score or scores occurred most often. Remember, when we have a near normal or reasonably symmetrical distribution, all three measures of central tendency are similar. In these cases, we typically use the mean to describe the data and, importantly, it is the measure of central tendency most often used when computing inferential statistics. However, when distributions are skewed, we should report both the mean and the median. This tells the reader of the research report that the data are skewed and provides information to estimate the center of the distribution.

Measures of Variation

Look back at Figure 10.1. It provides two types of information. First, it provides information about where the middle of the distribution is, our measures of central tendency. Second, it provides information on the spread of scores, or how much they vary from one another. Although there are a variety of *measures of variation,* we consider only the two that are most common to clinical research—range and standard deviation.

Range. Again, look back at Figure 10.1 and Table 10.1. They show that our smallest score is 65 and our largest score is 77. The difference between these scores is the range. The formula for computing the range is $R = H - L + 1$, where R = range, H = highest score, and L = lowest score. We add 1 because the simple subtraction of low from high excludes the highest score from being included in the outcome. For the data in Figure 10.1 and Table 10.1, the range would be $R = 77 - 65 + 1$, or 13. Unfortunately, the range is a rather crude measure of variability, especially when distributions are highly skewed.

Standard Deviation. The standard deviation is a statistic of great importance for both descriptive and inferential statistics. Before we describe its uses, let's see how it is calculated. The formula for deriving a standard deviation is $SD = \sqrt{\Sigma (\bar{X} - Xi)^2 / N - 1}$. For the purpose of illustration, consider the following data set: 1, 2, 3, 4, 5, 6, and 7 (and also see Table 10.3). From our previous discussion, we can calculate the mean ($\bar{X}$) of this data. It is 4. Okay, now each of the individual scores (Xi) varies by some amount from the mean. For example, 1 is three units from the mean ($4 - 1 = 3$), 2 is two units from the mean ($4 - 2 = 2$), and so on. Similarly, 7 is three units from the mean ($4 - 7 = -3$). When we sum the differences of all our scores ($\bar{X} - Xi$) we get a score of 0. So, in order to be able to go farther in calculating the standard deviation, we need to get rid of the minus signs associated with some of the difference scores. Because the square of a negative number is a positive number, we simply square each difference score ($\bar{X} - Xi)^2$.

The next step is to sum the squares of the difference scores [$\Sigma (\bar{X} - Xi)^2$]. This is called the *sum of squares.* Here we get a total of 28. Now to obtain our standard deviation, we need to divide by $N - 1$, where N = the number of scores. This statistic is called the *degrees of freedom,* or the number of units of possible variation. Based on our data we have $7 - 1 = 6$ degrees of

Table 10.3   Sample Data, Including Mean (X) and Difference Scores (X – Xi) for Calculating Standard Deviation

Xi	$\overline{X}$	$\overline{X}$ – Xi	$(\overline{X} - Xi)^2$
1	4	3	9
2	4	2	4
3	4	1	1
4	4	0	0
5	4	–1	1
6	4	–2	4
7	4	–3	9

freedom. Okay, so far we have $\Sigma (\overline{X} - Xi)^2/N = 28/7 = 4$. Our *variance* score is 4. But, because we squared all of our numbers to get rid of the minus signs, we need to take the square root of our variance score. This is the final step in calculating our standard deviation. When we take the square root of our variance score we obtain a standard deviation of 2.

Now you know how to compute the standard deviation (without relying on your computer program to do so). What is so important about this statistic? How is it used in descriptive and inferential statistics? The standard deviation divides any normally distributed set of data into categories that occupy an equal distance on the X-axis (horizontal line). Illustration 10.2 provides an example of a normal distribution of data along with information pertinent to standard deviation. The figure shows that 34.1% of all scores fall between the mean and one standard deviation. This is true for scores that are one standard deviation above or below the mean. Scores that are below the mean are represented by negative standard deviations (i.e., less than the mean), and those above the mean are represented by positive standard deviations (i.e., more than the mean). Furthermore, 13.6% of the scores fall between 1 and 2 standard deviations, 2.1% fall between 2 and 3 standard deviations, and so on. The percentages in each category are true for all normally distributed data and, in such cases, 99.6% of data will be within 3 standard deviations of either side of the mean.

Why is this important for describing a distribution of scores? Consider that the data in Illustration 10.2 represent information derived using one of the several IQ tests that have a mean of 100 and a standard deviation of 15. In this case, we can see that fewer than 16% of the population have IQ scores greater than 115. We can also see that approximately 2% of the population would have IQ scores lower than 70. This detail of description provides a better understanding of the data than simply reporting a measure of central tendency or range.

Illustration 10.2. Normal Distribution Showing Mean ($\bar{X}$) and Standard Deviation (SD)

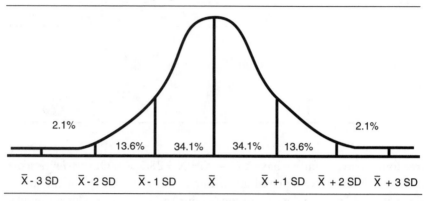

Summary

Descriptive statistics are very useful for summarizing a set of data. They can provide convenient numbers that can tell us how participants performed on average and how much variation there was in their scores. Descriptive statistics are, however, limited as to what they can tell us about a set of data. They are further limited in that they can't inform us to any significant degree about how similar or different two or more sets of data are. The ability to state with exactness the degree of similarity or difference between data sets is a keystone of most clinical research; so, we now turn our attention to some basic inferential statistics that allow us to make such determinations.

Inferential Statistics

Here we describe some statistical procedures used for determining if data collected from two or more groups differ in a statistically meaningful manner. We also describe how we can determine if data on two or more sets of variables are meaningfully related (or correlated) with one another. However, before doing so, we need to take a look at one of the primary methods by which clinical researchers determine how meaningful these differences and relationships are—the concept of *statistical probability*.

Estimating Probability

Perhaps the most commonly used, and most often misused, statistic in inferential statistics is the *p* value. In Chapter 3 we mentioned that the *p* value is a measure of the likelihood that your results could have occurred by chance. In other words, the *p* value (or, more succinctly, *p*) indicates the probability that your findings do not represent true differences between the phenomena you are studying.

In Chapter 1 we described a study conducted by two third-grade teachers on computer keyboarding skills. In that study the teachers first measured how fast and accurately their Grade 3 students from two separate classes could type. They found that before keyboarding training their students could accurately type slightly more than two words per minute. Next, one class was allowed to use the computer during a period of class time but did not receive specific instruction in keyboarding. The other class worked on a computer program that taught 10-finger typing skills. At the end of the study, the teachers again measured typing skills. They found that the children who had not received training in typing skills improved little in their typing speed, still typing only slightly more than three words per minute. On the other hand, those who had received training were typing, on average, more than seven words per minute. This sounds good. Now, an important question is, "Is this difference due to the training, or lack thereof, in keyboarding skills, or could these difference have occurred just by chance?" With the data we have provided you, the correct answer is, "I don't know."

In order for us to state with confidence that the differences are meaningful, we must resort to statistical tests of significance. We describe examples of statistical tests later in this section. For purposes of our discussion of probability, we need now to turn our attention to the concept of *random error*. In any research study a certain amount of random error occurs. It can arise when we have not been able to control all extraneous (or nuisance) variables, as described in Chapter 9. In clinical research, random error is a common problem because it is so difficult to control participants' feelings, memories, and the like. A few examples should help clarify the concept.

Consider flipping a coin. If we flip a coin 10 times and count the number of heads and tails, we would expect to get five heads and five tails. If you flip the coin in an unbiased manner a sufficiently large number of times, this is what you would get. However, on any one set of 10 flips you may get four heads and six tails or, indeed, some other combination. This variance is random error due to chance. Now consider feelings of depression. If we asked a person to estimate how depressed he or she is at one point in time, we would get one estimate. If we asked the same person to estimate his or her level of depression a week later, we might get a different estimate depending on what had happened to the person during the intervening week. The difference in estimates could be real (i.e., due to a change in mood) or it could be due to random error, stemming from variables unrelated to mood (e.g., being tired from reading this text, not attending closely to the questions). When we make probability estimates of chance, we are attempting to determine if the differences between our groups could have occurred by chance or random error.

For simple tests of differences between groups, clinical researchers generally accept that that if p is less than 5%, then it can be assumed that the results are likely not due to chance. The notation "$p < .05$" tells us that our findings could have occurred by chance fewer than 5 times in 100. This means that if we performed an experiment 100 times, we could expect to find no statistical differences between groups in less than 5 of the experiments. If our analysis shows that the results were not likely due to chance factors, we can say they are *significant at the .05 level*. Oftentimes, researchers may use more stringent p values, for example, accepting the probability of chance findings only 1 out of 100 ($p < .01$) or 1 out of 500 ($p < .005$) instances.

One of the major problems with the use of p is that only small differences between means may produce statistically significant results, yet in other circumstances the same mean differences may not provide significant results. This can occur when sample sizes differ from one circumstance or study to another. This can be a problem for clinical researchers because, in the case of larger samples, we may obtain statistically significant results that are clinically meaningless or, in other words, do not have clinical significance (see Illustration 10.3). Consider a situation in which we give 1,000 depressed people a new antidepressant and another 1,000 depressed people a placebo. When we analyze our data—in this case, obtained from a measure of depression—we may find that the medication group shows reductions in scores that are, according to our p, significantly greater than the reductions observed in the placebo group. However, the difference may only be a few points less and, although it may achieve statistical significance, it may have little clinical significance. If the medication is to be of use to patients, it should produce a more profound reduction in depression (and, thus, scores on our depression measure). The point here is that, although statistical significance is important, the clinical researcher needs also to attend to clinical significance.

Determining Whether Data Are Significantly Different

Using inferential statistics we can determine with statistical certainty if participants who receive two (or more) different treatments actually produce different results. There are two main categories of statistical tests of this type—parametric and nonparametric. The two differ in several respects but,

Illustration 10.3. Understanding Clinical Significance

Clinical researchers need to be concerned with both statistical and clinical significance. If our research is evaluating factors important and meaningful to the lives of people, we should strive to show that our findings are not only statistically important, but that they are clinically meaningful. Fortunately, there are several methods for evaluating clinical significance. For example, one can evaluate differences in percentages of people whose scores return to a normal range on some measure of importance following treatment. If a greater proportion of the scores of those in the treatment group return to normal when compared to those in the control group, then we have a good indicator that our treatment was clinically significant. This method of evaluating clinically significant change is very useful when we have good normative data for our measures. A good example of this method of evaluating clinical significance was Nezu and Perri's (1989) study on the effectiveness of two types of problem-solving methods to treat depression. They found that 87.5% of their patients who received the full problem-solving condition had scores within the normal range of the Beck Depression Inventory compared to 50% who received an abbreviated form of the treatment.

most important, *parametric statistics* are based on the assumption that your data are (a) continuous (rather than discrete, or categorical) and (b) normally distributed. On the other hand, *nonparametric statistics* do not require normally distributed data. This class of statistics generally compares rank orders of data in comparison groups. For example, if participants in Group A had scores of 35, 30, and 32 on the Beck Depression Inventory, and those in Group B had scores of 29, 25, and 30, Group A would have two participants with higher-ranking scores than participants in Group B. For all practical purposes the scores could be converted into ranks of 6 for the highest score (i.e., 35 in our example) and 1 for the lowest score (i.e., 25 in our example).

Despite some advantages of nonparametric statistics, it is parametric statistics that are, by far, the most commonly used by researchers. There are two primary reasons for this. First, they generally permit more complex analyses. Second, they have been better researched and, as a result, their properties are better known. For the remainder of this section we focus on providing an overview of parametric statistics, starting with the simple and moving to the more complex. Those interested in exploring nonparametric statistics further may wish to consult textbooks such as *Nonparametric Statistics in Health Care Research: Statistics for Small Samples and Unusual Distributions* (Pett, 1997).

t tests. *t* tests (the *t* is always written in the lower case for this type of statistic) are used to compare data from one group against (a) a population mean, (b) data from another independent group, or (c) data from the same group at another time. This, in the simplest terms, is a statistic that is based on the standard deviation obtained from the scores of each group and weighted by the number of participants in each group. However, despite these types of *t* tests being calculated using similar procedures, there are important differences in the way the pooled standard deviation is determined. Because the first two types are based on two groups of participants versus only one group compared to itself in the third type, the number of participants entered into the formula for calculating the standard deviation differs for each. Let's look at examples of each of these applications of the *t* test.

Consider fictional data from a national survey conducted during the late 1990s indicating that children aged 5 to 7 watch an average of 4 hours of television daily (remember, this is fictional data). We wondered if this was true of children whose parents were university professors. Maybe these children would be more interested in academic pursuits such as reading. Thus, we randomly selected 25 children whose parents taught at a local university and measured the amount of time they watched television. We found that they watched an average of only 2.5 hours of television daily. Now, if we knew the standard deviation of the survey data, we could test to see if professors' children watched significantly less television than did children in the national survey. To do this type of analysis, we compare data that we collect from a sample of interest to that obtained, under similar circumstances, from the same general population.

As noted above, a *t* test can also be used to compare results obtained from two independent samples that have received different treatments. Ideally, the members in each condition would have been assigned to their group in a random manner. In this type of situation, we might compare scores on a measure of social anxiety given to 30 people with Social Anxiety Disorder who receive a 10-week cognitive-behavioral program to a group of 30 people with the same diagnosis who receive general counseling. Knowing the mean, standard deviation, and number of participants for each group allows us to perform the *t* test. This type of *t* test is called an *independent samples t test* or a *between-groups t test* because we are considering data collected from independent samples.

Finally, let's imagine that we are interested in determining if a group of students who receive special training in language skills improves over the course of training. We would measure their language skills at the beginning and then again at the completion of training. We could then compare their scores collected at the start to those collected at the end of the program. Again, knowing the mean, standard deviation, and number of participants for each group allows us to perform the *t* test. In this case the statistic is called a *dependent samples t test* or a *within-groups t test* because the results are dependent on the same group of participants. Later we will show you that between- and within-groups analyses can be combined in more complex statistical procedures.

Analysis of Variance (ANOVA). Sometimes we want to compare more than two groups of participants. For example, we may wish to compare the effects of several doses of a medication for Alzheimer's disease to determine if there are dose-related differences in performance on a test of short-term recall. We might give one group of randomly selected patients a placebo, another group 25 milligrams, and a third group 50 milligrams of the medication for 30 days. We would then reevaluate recall performance. Technically, we could analyze our recall data with a series of independent *t* tests where we compare Group 1 with Group 2, Group 1 with Group 3, and then Group 2 with Group 3. However, there are difficulties with this type of analysis. Doing three separate tests increases the chances of getting one or more significant finding due to random error. One way to control for this would be to adjust *p* to account for the increase in random error by dividing *p* by the number of tests. So, in this case, $p = .05/3 = .016$.

There are, however, statistical tests that are designed to be used with more than two groups or conditions. One such test is called analysis of variance (ANOVA). An ANOVA is simply a robust *t* test that gives a researcher the opportunity to derive much more information. ANOVAs and *t* tests are based on the same theoretical linear model of calculating sums of squares and standard deviations but, in ANOVA, the method of calculating sums of squares and standard deviations is much more complex because of combining the scores from several groups.

To illustrate the advantages of ANOVAs over simple *t* tests, let's consider the example described above comparing three dose levels of a new medication for Alzheimer's disease. In addition to determining if there are dose-related responses, we might wish to see if there are differences in response to the medications as a function of sex. Now we have a design that includes the levels of medication (placebo, 25 mg, and 50 mg) and two levels of sex (male and female). This is referred to as a 3 (dose level) × 2 (sex) design. Based on the analysis of this design we can obtain information about (a) differences in dose level, collapsed across both males and females, and (b) differences between men and women, collapsed across dose level. The phrase *collapsed across* simply means that we combine the scores of the collapsed condition. For example, when we collapse across the medication condition we are comparing the scores of men and women regardless of which level of medication they received. The statistical information from each collapsed condition is referred to as a *main effect*. So, in this case, we would be able to determine if patients receiving the different medication doses differed significantly from each other on recall performance (and, if so, we would say there was a main effect of dose) *and* if male and female patients differed significantly on recall performance (in which case, we would say there was a main effect of sex).

But, the true beauty of using an ANOVA when you have more than one condition of interest is that not only can you obtain information about main effects, but you can also see how each condition *interacts* with the other. In our example, we may find that dose and sex interact. That is, it may be that the best therapeutic effect (i.e., the best performance on our recall test) for males is at the 50 mg dose, whereas the optimal effect for females might be with the 25 mg dose.

There is yet another advantage to using ANOVA. It permits us to combine both between-group and within-group measures. So, we could expand our medication study to include measures of recall performance within the same group of participants obtained at different times, say before treatment, after 4 weeks of treatment, and again after 16 weeks of treatment. This would permit us to see if there are differential changes across time as a function of dose level and sex. This would give us a 3 (dose level) × 2 (sex) × 3 (assessment time) design. The first two levels would be between participants, and the third—assessment time—a within-participant component.

Although ANOVAs permit us to obtain much more information than we could ever get using *t* tests, there are several complications. First, with each condition we add, we must increase the number of participants in order to have adequate statistical power to detect real differences between groups or conditions. Second, the greater the number of conditions we have, the greater the difficulty in interpreting the results, especially the interactions. Although interpreting the interaction between dose and sex (called a two-way interaction) in the example above is relatively simple and straightforward, it would be more difficult to interpret if assessment time also entered the interaction (a three-way interaction). If we were to consider the influence of yet another factor, say type of dementia (Alzheimer's disease vs. senile dementia of Lewy body type), and it entered the significant (now four-way) interaction, things would become very difficult to tease apart.

Summary. *t* tests and ANOVAs are quite common in clinical research. They allow us to make important inferences about differences between groups (or within the same group across assessment time) far more reliably than if we relied solely on descriptive statistics.

Table 10.4   Exercises and Stress Data

Participant	Exercise (hours/week)	Stress Level
1	1	12
2	7	7
3	4	6
4	6	8
5	9	2
6	5	5
7	3	9
8	0	4
9	2	10
10	8	1

Determining Whether Data Are Significantly Related

Thus far, most of our examples have focused on exposing two or more groups of participants to different manipulations or treatments and seeing if these produce different results. Sometimes we may have a quite different interest. Indeed, we may want to know how related the data from two or more conditions are. We can determine relatedness using a number of statistics. Below we provide an overview of the most common ones.

The Correlation Coefficient. The most commonly used statistic of relatedness is the Pearson product-moment correlation, or r. Let's look at an example of where we might wish to calculate r. Imagine that we are interested in determining if there is a relationship between the amount of time people spend exercising and their level of stress. Okay, further assume that we have reliable and valid measures of exercise and stress and that, for both measures, increasing scores indicate increased levels of the variable being measured. Now, we ask 10 randomly selected co-workers to complete our measures of exercise and stress. We obtain the data shown in Table 10.4. Based on these data, do you think there is a relationship between exercise and stress?

Let's look at the data in a different format. Figure 10.3 shows the same data plotted such that a single point is used to describe each co-worker's exercise score on the Y-axis and stress level on the X-axis. Look at the pattern. The line drawn through the data points is called the *regression line*. The regression line is computed to minimize the distance from each score to the line or, in other words, to provide the best fit. The slope of the line is an indicator of the degree of relationship between two variables. The steeper the slope, the greater the degree of relationship. A *positive correlation* exists when an increase in one variable is associated with an increase

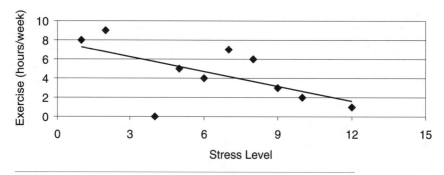

Figure 10.3.   Exercise and Stress Level Data With Regression Line

in the other. A *negative correlation* exists when an increase in one variable is associated with a decrease in the other. The flatter the slope, the smaller the relationship between the two variables. If the slope is flat, there is no correlation between the variables. The degree of relationship between two variables, as measured by the correlation coefficient, can vary from $r = 1.0$ to $r = -1.0$. Negative values represent negative correlations.

As you can see from our data, there appears to be a negative correlation between the number of hours exercised and level of stress. When we calculated the correlation coefficient we found that $r = -.60$. But, is the correlation between amount of exercise and stress levels statistically significant? Our p value was $p = .07$. As you will remember from our discussion of estimates of probability, this means that we could expect to get these results by chance 7 out of 100 times that we assess the relationship between stress and exercise levels. Because this exceeds our acceptable p of .05, even if by only a slight margin, we conclude that the relationship is not significant. If we had a larger sample, say 50 participants, and found the same correlation of $-.60$, it would be significant (at about $p < .001$). Remember, the more participants, the less the random error and more reliable the data.

Regression. We can use the correlation coefficient to tell us how much common variance is shared by two variables. If exercise and stress levels were perfectly correlated ($r = -1.0$), it would not be necessary to measure both variables. Because they have perfectly shared variance, knowing how many hours a person exercised would tell us how stressed the person was. In our hypothetical study, a score on our exercise variable was a moderate predictor of stress levels—they shared a moderate amount of variance. We can compute the amount of variance shared by two correlated variables by squaring the r. When we use the square of the correlation coefficient to estimate the amount of shared variance, the symbol R^2 is used. For our data the $R^2 = .60^2 = .36$. This means that for our data set, 36% of the variance of stress can be accounted for by knowing how many hours each person exercised. If our correlation between exercise and stress levels had been $r = -.90$, the shared variance would have been $R^2 = .81$, or 81%. Thus, the more highly two variables are correlated, the more we can predict one score by knowing the other.

In our example, we stated that the line of best fit, or regression line, provided a good visual indicator for how related two variables are. The regression line is derived mathematically and can be used not only to provide a best fit, but also to predict scores when only one of our variables is known. If our data had been reliable (and, ideally, we had a higher correlation), and if we knew that Mary was an exercise nut, working out at least 10 hours per week, we could, using the regression formula, predict her stress score. Correlational analyses, therefore, when properly used can show not only the degree of relatedness between two variables, but can be used to make predictions about one variable based on a known score on another variable that is highly correlated with the unknown score.

Multiple Regression and Related Analyses. When we correlate two variables we can determine how accurately a score on one variable can predict a score on a second variable. But, quite often, numerous factors contribute such that a variable, like stress, can be more accurately predicted by more than one variable. It is very likely that we could greatly improve on our prediction of stress if we were to add measures of job satisfaction and frequency of daily hassles to our measure of exercise. If we did this, we would employ a statistical procedure called *multiple regression* to analyze our data. Multiple regression permits us, through correlational analyses, to use several variables (called *predictor variables*) at the same time to predict scores on a variable of interest (often called the *criterion variable*). There are many different applications of multiple regression analyses, including standard approaches, sequential approaches, and stepwise approaches, all of which tell us slightly different things and are used under different circumstances. Unfortunately, it is beyond the scope or intent of this chapter to review the distinctions between these approaches. We recommend that you refer to the text by Tabachnick and Fidell (1996), mentioned above, for a thorough review of multiple regression.

It is also noteworthy that there are numerous other statistical techniques, equally important to clinical researchers for purposes of model building and testing, that are based on the concepts of multiple regression. These techniques include path analysis and structural equation modeling. In Chapter 4 we mentioned a study in which we found that a predisposition to be fearful

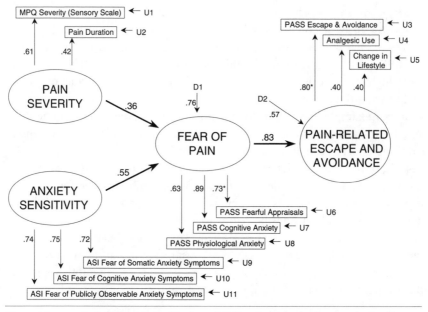

Figure 10.4.   Path Diagram for Final Model Showing Standardized Path Coefficients for Significant Paths (all $ps < .001$).

SOURCE: From "Role of Anxiety Sensitivity in Pain-Related Fear and Avoidance," by G. J. G. Asmundson and S. Taylor, 1996, *Journal of Behavioral Medicine, 19*, p. 582. Copyright 1996 by Plenum Publishing Corporation. Reprinted by permission.

NOTE: Coefficients marked with an asterisk were fixed to identify the model. D = disturbance terms. U = uniqueness terms.

was predictive of fear of pain and escape avoidance behavior in people with chronic pain (Asmundson & Taylor, 1996). We were able to make this determination only by testing the model shown in Figure 10.3. This type of testing, although somewhat complex, is gaining greater use in the realm of clinical research. For detailed coverage of these statistics, we recommend that you refer to texts such as *Principles and Practice of Structural Equation Modeling* (Kline, 1998) and *Basic Principles of Structural Equation Modeling: An Introduction to LISREL and EQS* (Mueller, 1996).

Summary. Correlational analyses are used to assess the degree of relatedness and variance shared between variables. More complex statistical techniques, such as multiple regression and various modeling procedures, allow us to answer questions regarding the association among a larger number of potential predictors of a variable of interest.

Summary

The purpose of this chapter was to (re)acquaint you with basic concepts of statistics so that you can better apply them to (a) your data analyses and (b) your critical evaluation of the research articles that you read. As mentioned, statistics is often one of the most challenging aspects of the whole clinical research enterprise. The concepts we discussed should assist in creating, or reestablishing, a solid foundation from which you can proceed. But do consult with your mentor or a hired consultant if need be (and funds permitting), particularly when planning or interpreting more complex statistics. And, no, we have not forgotten our consideration of Julia Roberts's smile width. To determine if her smile is unusually wide, you would need to know how it compared to your sample data. According to tabloid data, her smile width measures in at 80 mm. Is it unusually wide? Check back and see. Now, does this tell you anything about her appeal or is more information needed? At this point, we hope that you can go back to determine what additional data are needed and, thereafter, how to analyze them to answer this question. If so, we have accomplished our objective.

References

Asmundson, G. J. G., & Taylor, S. (1996). Role of anxiety sensitivity in pain-related fear and avoidance. *Journal of Behavioral Medicine, 19,* 573–582.

Coolidge, F. L. (2000). *Statistics: A gentle introduction.* Thousand Oaks, CA: Sage.

Gravetter, F. J., & Wallnau, L. B. (1999). *Statistics for the behavioral sciences* (5th ed.). Stamford, CT: Wadsworth.

Grimm, L. G. (1993). *Statistical applications for the behavioral sciences.* New York: John Wiley.

Kline, R. B. (1998). *Principles and practice of structural equation modeling.* New York: Guilford.

Mueller, R. O. (1996). *Basic principles of structural equation modeling: An introduction to LISREL and EQS* (S. Fienberg & I. Olkin, Eds.). New York: Springer Texts in Statistics.

Nezu, A. M., & Perri, M. G. (1989). Social problem-solving therapy for unipolar depression: An initial dismantling investigation. *Journal of Consulting and Clinical Psychology, 57,* 408–413.

Pett, M. A. (1997). *Nonparametric statistics in health care research: Statistics for small samples and unusual distributions.* Thousand Oaks, CA: Sage.

Tabachnick, B. G., & Fidell, L. S. (1996*). Using multivariate statistics* (3rd ed.). New York: HarperCollins.

PART III

Communicating Your Findings

11

Presenting Your Findings

So you've done all the work planning your study, conducting the research, and analyzing the results. Now you can kick back and relax. Right? Wrong!

Until you've communicated your research to others, your work is not done. Think back. What was the point of conducting the research in the first place? It was to find answers to important questions, correct? Well, that is surely not something you want to keep to yourself. The scientific process is not complete until you've presented your findings to others. Here's why and how to do it.

Why Present Your Research?

Your research needs to see the light of day. Although it may be personally satisfying to see the fruits of your labors (i.e., the results of your research), others need to see it, too. Why?

The Information Must Be Disseminated. If this was a research project worth doing, then it's a research project worth having others hear about. This is not to imply that all (or, for that matter, most) research will be of interest to the masses. More often than not, research advances are made in infinitesimally small steps. Your research is likely to be one of these steps (forward, we hope). As such, it may be of immediate interest only to others in your field. That's fine. These are the people who deserve to hear about it. If your results have more far-reaching implications, then your audience needs to be broader. Either way, if you keep the results to yourself, you're depriving the community at large from benefiting from your work. That violates both the spirit and, in the case of most government or foundation funded research, the letter of research principles.

Exceptions to the public's "right to know" exist, of course, in the case of research conducted by or for private agencies. In that case, it is generally accepted that the results of the research may have commercial implications (i.e., money could be made by selling the idea, process, or product) and that the agency has a right to protect its interests in this regard. This is the basis for patent protection. For example, a pharmaceutical company may fund a researcher at an academic institution to conduct a study to test a new medication for treating anxiety. Generally, it will have a contractual arrangement with the investigator and the institution, guaranteeing the confidentiality of the findings until it can assure that its intellectual property rights are safeguarded. Ultimately, though, the findings will need to be disseminated, even if solely for commercial purposes. Keeping a valuable secret hidden forever can only diminish its value.

The Results Must Be Verified. One of the dictums of science is that results must be replicated before they are believable. Even if you are the world's most cautious, careful researcher, and you replicated the results in your own laboratory a dozen times (in which case you may wish to see a mental health professional to determine if you have Obsessive Compulsive Disorder), your findings are considered tentative until others replicate them. Why? You may have made a mistake. (Yes, you may have made the same mistake a dozen times.) You may have studied an unusual sample of people (or rats), and your results may not generalize to more common settings. You may be lying. (Yes, unfortunately, fabrication does happen.) Until others can see what you've done, hear about how you've done it, judge it for themselves, and maybe try to do it themselves, your findings will not be widely accepted.

You Want Credit for the Findings. Let's say you find that combining essence of banana peel and extract of CD-ROMs provides a cure for slipped discs. Hurray! Back problems are a major source of pain and suffering. You've found a way to relieve a tremendous amount of suffering. Now you want others to know about it. For the reasons covered above (so others can try to verify your findings and replicate them, hopefully before people hear about it and start licking computer disks and before the banana futures market skyrockets). But for another reason, too. You want credit!

What do we mean by credit? It can mean actual ownership of the process or the product, in which case you need to run out and hire a lawyer to help you with the patent protection before you communicate your results. But credit also means making your peers aware of your accomplishments. This isn't boasting. This is taking public responsibility for your findings.

This is critical for professional advancement, particularly if you plan on an academic career. You might do great work, but if nobody hears about it, it's a waste of time and (usually someone else's) money. You receive professional credit for your work only when you present it to others and submit it to the scrutiny of your peers.

Where to Present Your Research

Where do you go about sharing your results with colleagues? There is no shortage of such opportunities. Below we highlight several of the more common ones.

Informal Presentations

Your first chance to share your findings is with colleagues in your laboratory or your department. Initially, this may be with other students or with your supervisor(s). The forum may be a once-weekly lab meeting where students are encouraged to present their works in progress. Or it may, literally, be in the hallway or over lunch. This is your opportunity to share results in their very early, not-yet-ready-for-prime-time, hot-off-the-presses (or, more likely, straight out of the computer) stage.

You should use these informal sharing opportunities with close peers to refine your ideas and test the validity of your assumptions. Too often, students are afraid to show their results to peers or supervisors until they are certain of their veracity. This is not necessary. If you think you've found something interesting, then let your immediate colleagues know. Ask their advice. Get them to tell you what you may have done wrong. And use their feedback to hone your experiment and make it better.

Presenting at Professional Conferences or Meetings

There are usually many opportunities to present in front of a wider audience of your peers. Chances are that there are several professional conferences or meetings each year that are relevant to your research. How do you find out about them? Ask your colleagues and supervisors. Check out the journals for your area of research; they usually list upcoming meetings of interest. Use Internet search engines. Then, probably with the help of your research mentor(s), decide on which of the meetings is most appropriate. The choice will depend on a number of factors, including the scientific caliber of the meeting, its anticipated theme or content, the likelihood of your research being accepted for presentation (this can vary widely between meetings), the locale, and even the cost of registration and attendance.

There are several customary formats for presenting results at professional meetings. These include

Posters. These are the meat-and-potatoes of most scientific meeting smorgasbords. They consist of, well, a poster, with the study objectives, methods, results, and conclusions succinctly highlighted, often with sensible use of graphs. Most meetings have poster sessions, where any number of posters are presented side by side for several hours. Presenters stand beside their posters, ready to explain their studies to and answer questions for passers-by. Meeting attendees will wander from poster to poster and will stop for longer periods of time at posters that interest them.

Though often viewed as less prestigious than oral presentations, probably because there are usually far fewer oral than poster presentations at each meeting, we love poster sessions because they provide a unique opportunity to interact with peers. They will come by, talk with you, ask you about your work, and maybe tell you about theirs (even if you didn't ask). Poster sessions are a great place to put faces to names ("Oh, are you Dr. McPherson of the McNeil-McPherson Basketball Evolutionary Theory? I thought you would be much taller!") and to make professional connections.

Research Papers and Symposia. Depending on the meeting, there are often several different formats for oral presentations. Individual research papers may be solicited and, if accepted, organized by the meeting program committee into topically related Paper Sessions. These might include anywhere from 3 to 10 papers, presented orally (usually with visual aids) for a specific time period (e.g., 20 minutes) with additional time (e.g., 5 minutes) for discussion and questions from the audience.

Another format is the research symposium, which typically involves a group of speakers selected by the symposium organizer (who is often also a speaker or discussant—the person who wraps things up at the end of the symposium) to address a particular topic. Typically, meetings will allot time slots (usually 60 to 120 minutes) for symposia and then permit researchers to submit their symposia to fill these slots. Symposia are generally more tightly thematically linked than research paper sessions. Often they are arranged to cover various aspects of a topic or, in some cases, to present opposing viewpoints.

Workshops or Roundtables. These vary in format and in intent. Workshops usually involve a group of participants getting together to review a topic, learn something new, or discuss an issue in depth. There may be a leader for the workshop, or it may be more free-form with everyone encouraged to share in the leadership. Some workshops are intended more as training sessions, in which case a workshop leader is clearly identified and an explicit curriculum developed in advance and followed throughout.

Roundtables typically involve a relatively small group of speakers, each of whom presents something formally (usually briefly) to the group, following which there is ample time for comment and discussion by other roundtable members and by the audience.

Choosing a Presentation Format

Once you've decided on which meeting you want to attend, how do you know which format to choose? Well, the first thing to do is to check the meeting's "Call for Papers." This is available by mail, upon request, or on the meeting's Web site. It should clearly indicate what presentation formats are available and how and when to apply (see Illustration 11.1). In some cases, there may be presentation tracks other than those specific to research and, though these often incorporate information gathered through the research process, they are typically geared to other audiences, such as those who suffer from a particular problem or those who treat it. If you miss the deadline, you're usually sunk. (Though it never hurts to check with the meeting organizers.)

If a variety of presentation formats are available, then ask yourself the following questions to help decide on an optimal format for your presentation:

Have I Done This Before? If this is your first time presenting at a scientific meeting, it might not be a bad idea to cut your teeth at a poster session before trying an oral presentation. But if you're feeling confident, and you've had experience thinking on your feet, then an oral presentation might be fine. Very often, a poster is the "default" submission. This means that if you submit an oral research paper, and it is not accepted because of a limited number of oral presentation slots, the organizers may offer you a poster slot instead. If this happens, say yes.

Is This a Hot Topic? If your research addresses a hot issue, something that is very topical for your field, you might want to organize a symposium.

Illustration 11.1. Example of Call for Papers

CALL FOR PAPERS
International Association of Arachidology 2002 Annual Conference
Peanut Butter Preferences in a Global Context
May 28 - 30, 2002
Smoothville Hotel
Crunchtown, CA

Over the past few decades there have been considerable strides made in understanding, managing, and treating indulgence in chunky peanut butter. Our knowledge of the preference for chunky peanut butter continues to grow. Through research, we extend the limits of what is known and refine our ability to intervene effectively. Please join us in 2002 as we take stock of the state-of-the-art in international peanut butter research, our history, the challenges ahead, and the implications of our growing knowledge to the well-being of those who prefer chunky.

Abstracts are invited for research symposia, research posters, and clinical workshops. Submissions are invited on any topic, as well as topics related specifically to this year's conference theme.

ABSTRACT: An abstract of 250 words or less is required for each proposal submitted. The abstract is a concise description of the specific purpose, content, methodology, results, and importance of the proposed presentation.

SUBMISSION DEADLINES
December 8, 2001

A. **RESEARCH PRESENTATIONS** include clinical or basic science studies pertaining to any aspect of chunky preference. Researchers wishing to present may submit in one of the following formats:
1)   Research Symposium
2)   Research Poster

1)   **Research Symposium**: These sessions focus on a specific topic in arachidology and represent several points of view. The proposer chairs the session, which includes up to four papers, a formal discussion, and a period for audience discussion.

2)   **Research Poster**: Submissions are invited on any subject relevant to arachidology. The poster format allows presenters and registrants to casually discuss research findings.

B. **CLINICAL WORKSHOPS** address a specific aspect of clinical practice. Any topic will be considered. Clinical workshops should be planned for 1 - 2 hours in length. Each abstract should be no more than 250 words in length and may be submitted by individuals or groups.

GENERAL INFORMATION

1.   The attached Abstract Submission Form should be used.

2.   Review the Submission categories to determine the appropriate format for the presentation.

3.   Complete one form for each submission.

4.   Type all copy.

5.   All presenters are required to register for the conference.

2002 Scientific Programme Committee

P. B. Brittle. Ph.D.. Programme Chair
Jiff P. B. Cookie. M.D.
Butter G. Cookie. Ph.D.. M.D.
I. Prefer Smooth. Ph.D.

Figure out (talk with your peers, check out the journals) who are the other investigators doing work in this area and contact several of them to participate in a symposium submission with you. Don't be shy about contacting experts in the field to participate; they are often willing and happy to do so. Assign each individual a topic (in consultation with them, of course), find a discussant (usually someone with a broad perspective on the field and/or very special expertise in this topic) if the meeting permits or encourages this, and submit the symposium as a "package" to the conference committee.

Is In-Depth Discussion of a Topic Desirable? If you feel that the field would benefit from detailed, more free-flowing discussion of a topic, then a workshop or roundtable might be the way to go. If your goal is to teach something new, then a workshop may fit best. If your goal is to provide a forum where thought leaders get things going and everyone participates, then a roundtable is probably just the thing.

Tips on Preparing an Effective Presentation

Once you have decided on a presentation format and have your work accepted for presentation, it will be necessary to prepare your materials for public consumption. Ideally, the goal here should be to make certain that the information you present is clear, concise, and easily digested within the context (presentation format) that you have selected. This sounds easy, but it may not be. Giving a good presentation requires preparation. Below we present some tips that may help you in preparing effective posters and oral presentations.

Posters

- *Know the format.* Find out (read the meeting information, check the Web site, or call the conference organizers if you're still not sure) about the size of the poster board. Poster boards are typically either 4 feet by 4 feet, or 4 feet high by 8 feet wide. But be sure. If your poster is too big, you'll wind up either offending your neighbor whose poster is half covered by yours. Or you'll find yourself with a pair of scissors, doing a last-minute poster trim.

- *Whole or pieces?* Posters come in different varieties, depending on how much money you want (or have) to spend on them. The most cost-effective mode is to use a laser or inkjet printer to print out separate sheets of paper, each containing the Abstract, Background, and other relevant sections of the presentation. These can then be thumb-tacked directly to the poster board or glued to a colored cardboard background and then tacked up. (Note, though, that pushpins and thumb tacks are becoming passé, replaced by Velcro strips that are attached to the back of the poster and adhere to a Velcro board. Be sure you know which is available at your meeting.) A more chic option is to have your poster professionally produced as a single unit (see Illustration 11.2). You bring the content to your friendly neighborhood (or university) printing service, and they create a single poster that rolls up in a tube. You then just unroll it, and tack (or Velcro) it up. This format is very elegant, but also tends to be very expensive.

- *Keep it simple.* Use point form, with items bulleted, wherever possible. If a graph or table can say it better than text, then go with the former. The tendency is to include *too much* information. You should generally include only the highlights,

saving the details for the journal publication. If people want more details, they'll ask you. Take another look at Illustration 11.2. What do you think? Is this poster simple enough? Or is there too much information? Well, in our opinion, this poster is close to ideal—its Introduction and Method are brief, and it makes use of graphics—but its Results and Discussion could be more succinct, and the text would be easier to follow if bulleted. Now take a look at Illustration 11.3. Here there is simply too much information.

- *Keep it large.*   Remember that interested people will walk by your poster, viewing it from distances of 3 feet or more. The title needs to be plainly visible. Moreover, the entire text of the poster, including the graphs or figures, should be legible from that distance. Use a large, dark, clean type font (e.g., 24 pt. or larger). There's no need to be too fancy. Simple use of color and spacing can add emphasis effectively.

- *Bring handouts.*   Most meetings encourage poster presenters to bring handouts. These are usually miniature versions of the poster that fit on a sheet of paper, although it is also acceptable to prepare a brief summary that contains additional detail. If you forget to bring handouts, get a piece of paper, a pen, and an envelope so that you have a convenient way of collecting the contact information of those who want you to send them a handout.

Oral Presentations

- *Know the format.*   How long is the time slot for your presentation? Are you permitted to talk for that entire time, or is part of it allotted to questions from the audience? Where will you be in the program? It is worth knowing whether others who precede you will have provided general introductions to the topic? If so, there is no need for you to go over the same ground. In fact, doing so can be redundant (and boring) for the audience.

- *Have proper equipment and materials.*   Be sure you have the right equipment available for any audiovisual aids you plan to use. Overhead and slide projectors are typically available, but some equipment needs to be arranged for in advance. For example, you will likely need to request a videocassette recorder if you plan to show film footage. If you plan to project slides from a computer, confirm whether one will be available with the requisite software (or indicate that you will bring your own), and request an LCD projector. Most important, be sure that you have your presentation materials with you, whether they are overheads, slides, computer disk, or whatever. We strongly recommend that you carry this material with you at all times while en route to the conference venue, particularly if flying. Do not pack your presentation materials in any luggage you are checking. This same rule applies to poster materials. Though this seems common sense, on more than one occasion one of us (years ago, of course) has had to do without slides that were packed in luggage that was lost by the airline.

- *Keep it short.*   Although 20 or 30 minutes—typical time slots for oral presentations—seem like a long time, they fly. Beginner speakers inevitably put too much material in their talk and run overtime. There is no better way to stress yourself out than to see the chairperson of the session waving a "2 minutes to go" card when you're

Illustration 11.3.   A Poster With Too Much Information

Factor Structure and Influence of Chronic Pain on Posttraumatic Stress Disorder Symptoms in Military Peacekeepers

Fiona D. Wright, Gordon J. G. Asmundson, Donald R. McCreary, and David Pedlar

University of Regina, Regina, Saskatchewan; Veterans Affairs Canada, Charlottetown, New Brunswick

Introduction

Recent evidence from factor analytic investigations of posttraumatic stress disorder (PTSD) symptoms have suggested that the symptom clusters outlined (re-experiencing of the event, avoidance and emotional numbing, and hyper-arousal) in current diagnostic criteria may not provide the best conceptualization of PTSD symptom structure. Additionally, findings have suggested that symptoms of chronic pain and symptoms of PTSD influence, and are potentially related to, one another. While the nature of the relationship between these two variables remains to be determined, it is important to consider whether PTSD symptom structure (see Figure 1) is associated with the presence of other symptoms that, like PTSD, impact on biological and cognitive state. These issues were addressed in this study using symptom data provided by male United Nations peacekeepers.

Method

In Study 1, participants were 400 (mean age 40.9 years; SD = 10.5) anonymous male United Nations peacekeepers from regular and reserve duty forces of the Canadian military who had been deployed overseas to a conflict theatre. As part of a health status assessment they completed measures of PTSD symptoms and general health status as well as socio-demographic and military service information.

In Study 2, participants were 787 anonymous male United Nations peacekeepers from those that participated in Study 1. They were divided into those with chronic back pain (CP; n = 427; mean age 40.9 years; SD = 10.4) and without (NCP; n = 341; mean age 40.8 years; SD = ...) chronic back pain on the basis of information provided about current pain experience and other health conditions.

Results

In Study 1, the results from the CFA indicated that the four-factor intercorrelated model provided the best fit to the data (S-B χ^2 = 1.69; IGFI = .91; AGFI = .87; CFI-R = .96; RMSEA = .07; SRMR = .05). Subsequently, in Study 2 the reliability of the four-factor intercorrelated model was examined in both the CP and NCP groups. The results, shown in Figures 2 and 3, suggested that the four-factor intercorrelated model for each group was somewhat different.

The multiple group comparisons showed that factor loadings varied significantly between the CP and NCP groups in two instances. These included significant differences on one (re-experiencing) item (item 5, having physical reactions when something reminded you of a stressful military experience?), two numbing items (item 11, feeling emotionally numb or being unable to have loving feelings for those close to you?; item 12, feeling as if your future will somehow be cut short?), and the primary hyper-arousal item (item 16, Being "superalert" (or watchful (or on guard?), and the magnitude of the factor loadings were higher in the CP group than the NCP group.

Discussion

The elevated magnitude of the factor loadings in the CP group suggests that chronic pain may have a cumulative negative impact upon the PTSD symptoms represented by these items. Indeed, physical reaction to reminders of the trauma, feeling emotionally numb, having a sense of foreshortened future, and being hypervigilant may become more salient (and likely further tap available coping resources) when one has co-occurring chronic pain.

However, while the differences are statistically significant, they may not be practically significant (i.e., the magnitudes of the factor loadings are relatively high) but the differences between them are small) with one exception - item 16, pertaining to hypervigilance. This implies that chronic pain most likely exerts influence on PTSD symptom structure and, by inference, underlying mechanisms, primarily by heightening hypervigilance.

The stability of the four-factor intercorrelated model implies that PTSD in military personnel may be viewed as an amalgam of four related but discrete mechanisms. The influence of chronic pain on both symptom presentation and structure, particularly as it pertains to hypervigilance startle, further suggests that careful assessment and treatment of chronic pain symptoms may assist in successful resolution of the posttraumatic stress responses of these patients.

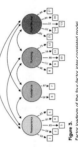

Figure 1.
Simplified factor models tested using confirmatory factor analysis: hierarchical two-factor model; four-factor intercorrelated model; and hierarchical four-factor model.

Figure 2.
Factor loadings of the four-factor inter-correlated model for the chronic back pain group. Item(s) cross loading on another factor are marked with an asterisk.

Figure 3.
Factor loadings of the four-factor inter-correlated model for the group without chronic pain. Item(s) cross loading on another factor are marked with an asterisk.

only halfway through your talk. So plan your talk. Then cut it in half and take it from there. A good rule of thumb is to use no more than one slide for every minute of speaking time. So a 30-minute time slot, where 10 minutes are allocated for questions and answers, means 20 minutes of speaking time and no more than 20 slides!

- *Keep it simple.* Novices tend to put too much information on each slide. A good rule of thumb is to have each slide say no more than two things. (One is better.) These are best presented in point form, as bulleted text. Have a look at Illustration 11.4 and decide which you would find more useful while sitting and listening to a presentation. Figures, pie and bar graphs (rather than tables, which 90% of the time have text that is too small for the audience to read), or other images should liberally be used as much as possible instead of text. Mixing text and figures helps to captivate and keep the audience's attention.

- *Practice.* Ask a few colleagues to sit and listen to your talk. Ask for their critical feedback. Time the talk. Then make changes as necessary to keep the talk as lively, brief, and clear as possible. Practice and time it again. Through repeated iterations of this process you will not only nail down your timing but, also, you will become intimately familiar with the "feel" of your talk, your slides, and the audience response to your presentation.

Disclosure of Financial Interests or Other Affiliations

It is important that you be open with the readers of your poster or the listeners to your talk about any financial interests you may have with regard to the topic under consideration. For example, if you are a shareholder in the company whose product you are discussing, you want the audience to know. This does not mean that your work is biased—this would be a serious ethical violation—but you want listeners to be able to make their own judgments. Similarly, if you are (or have been in the recent past) a paid consultant for a company whose product is mentioned in your presentation—even if you are not a consultant for that particular product—you want to disclose this affiliation. If you're unsure if your financial or other ties are sufficient to warrant disclosure, then err on the side of disclosing. An example of a disclosure, to come at the beginning of a lecture, would be, "Before I begin, I want to mention that I am a paid consultant for the Better Living Through Drugs Pharmaceutical Company, and that they provided funding for this research project."

Summary

Presenting your findings to an audience of your peers is a necessary part of the research endeavor. Doing this informally is an ideal way to refine your ideas, bounce possibilities off your colleagues, and fix potential problems before your findings are ready for prime time. Formal presentations at

Illustration 11.4.   Examples of Slides With Appropriate (top) and Too
Much (bottom) Information

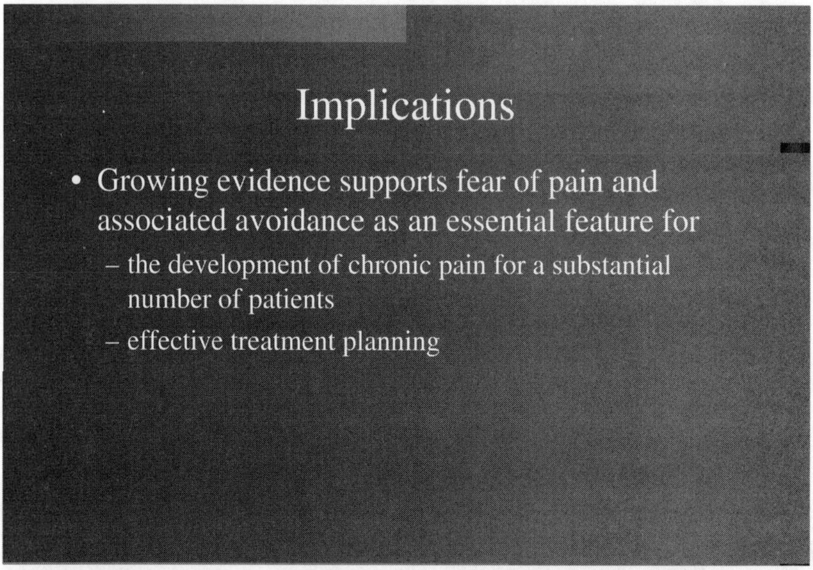

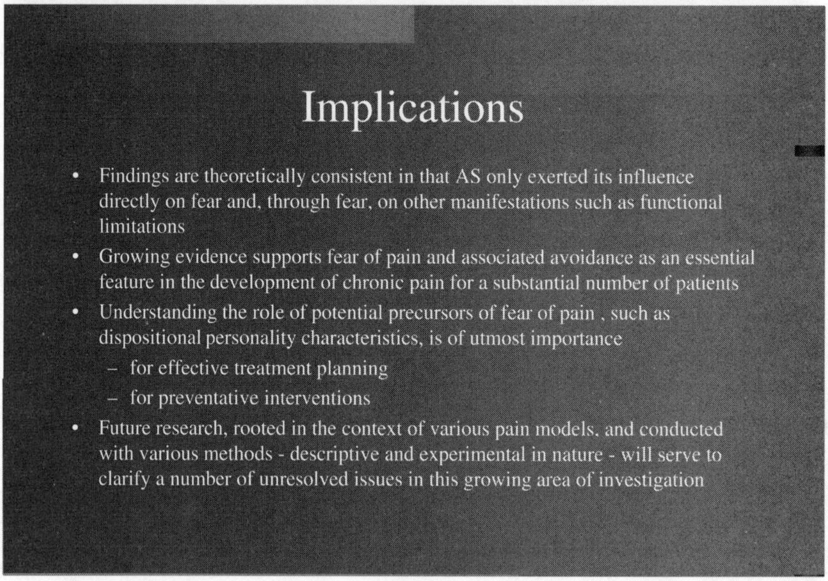

scientific meetings provide the forum for your work to be known, and for
your reputation to be established, by your peers world-round. Presenting in
front of well-known scientists in your field can be intimidating and downright

frightening. Don't let this stop you. Keep in mind that they all were in your position at one time, and most of them (unfortunately, not all) remember that. Expect to have your work critiqued and criticized. Much of the criticism will be constructive, well-intended, and immensely valuable. Take it in that spirit, and learn from it to make the next major milestone for your findings—their publication in a professional journal—that much better.

12

On Writing and Publishing

Publish or perish! No kidding. It's the academic way of life. Get used to it. And learn how to thrive in it if you so decide.

A sage mentor once told one of us, "Research is a business and publications are its currency." Sounds harsh, but it's true. Your success as a researcher, at least in the world of academia, will be judged by the quality—and though we hate to admit it—the quantity of your publications. Publishing an article in a peer-reviewed journal is the penultimate sharing of your findings with the world. Oral or poster presentations at meetings often precede publication—and feedback obtained from these sessions may help shape the nascent manuscript—but journal publication is the bottom line. Even outside of traditional academic settings, such as in the corporate research world, publications are highly valued. A publication about a new product or discovery in a top journal can bring attention that translates into increased shareholder interest, augmented sales, and, ultimately, more dollars. Likewise, to the clinician, publication about a treatment strategy can raise credibility with treatment seekers and insurance providers.

For all these reasons, it is imperative that scientists become skilled at writing and publishing. (The two endeavors, though linked, are not synonymous. More about this later.) It must be acknowledged that not all great researchers are great writers. The converse is certainly no less true. We know of brilliant scientists who couldn't put two words together. So what did they do? Some struggled to get their careers on track; some never made it. Others sought out mentors who could teach them how to write and, over time, improved their writing dramatically. And others reached the point in their careers where they were able to hire professional science writers to do it for them. Most of us don't have this luxury, though, so we must do the best we can. (Some, including ourselves, actually enjoy writing and wouldn't think of turning over this final piece of the creative process to a hired gun.)

Why Good Work Goes Unpublished (And What to Do About It)

It has been our experience that many students present their research findings at meetings, yet fail to take the next step and publish their findings. Why does this happen? There are a number of possible reasons.

Time and Place. It is common for a student to complete a piece of research, present it at a professional meeting, and then move on to a doctoral or post-doctoral position (or a real job) in another locale. The motivation to publish the work may diminish as the temporal and geographic distance from the study and the laboratory where it was conducted grow. People get busy. Other responsibilities supervene. And good work often goes unpublished.

How can you prevent this travesty? Promise yourself when you defend your dissertation or present your findings at a meeting that you'll take the next step and try to publish your work. Better yet, make that same promise to your mentor or supervisor and ask him or her to hold you to it!

Fear of Failure. Many people never try to publish their work because they are afraid it will be rejected. So, rather than risk failure, they avoid success altogether by never submitting their work for publication.

These timid souls don't know the two secrets of publishing that we will share with you now. (Please don't disclose these secrets to people who haven't bought this book. They're simply too valuable to give away for free.) Write them in your diary, tap them excruciatingly slowly into your electronic organizer (we'll wait), tattoo them on your arm, and sear them forever into your memory. Here they are:

Secret #1: Everyone gets rejected.

Secret #2: (Almost) everyone eventually gets published.

All of us have had fantastic, earth-shattering (an opinion not shared by the reviewers) research rejected by the first and best journal we sent it to. Though we are loathe to admit it, this has happened more than once. For those of us who have been in the research business for a while, it has happened many times. The only people who never get their manuscripts rejected are those who never submit them for publication.

What many novices fail to realize is that rejection in writing is rarely absolute. There are many professional venues for publication. In the broad field of psychological research, for example, there are hundreds of journals. (See "How to Pick a Journal" later in this chapter.) Though one may reject your manuscript—often not because it's awful but because there are many manuscripts competing for limited page space—another may embrace it avidly. Try not to let yourself be demoralized by a rejection. Read the referees' comments, see how you can improve the paper by following their lead, make changes, and submit it elsewhere. (We will say more later in this chapter about how to handle letters of rejection.)

Procrastination. Lack of time, lack of motivation, and fear of failure may be at the core of procrastination. But, it is our experience that it is often unknowable why some students endlessly put off writing and submitting their work for publication. So our motto is, "Procrastination: Just don't do it!" One of our mentors had a note taped to his office door that read, "Unlike wine, data do not get better with age." How true! If your work was even remotely topical when you started it, chances are it's still relevant— and worth publishing—by the time you've finished it. But the longer you wait, the greater the likelihood that your findings will have become trivial, uninteresting, or redundant. If this was the fear that led you to procrastinate in the first place, it will have become a self-fulfilling prophecy.

Writing a Manuscript for Peer Review

Okay, you've sidestepped procrastination, writer's block, and other obstacles, and you're ready to go. Where do you start?

Pick a Target Journal. Decide where you'd like to see your findings published. Then do a reality check and aim for a journal that has a reasonable likelihood of accepting your submission. Early in your research career, you are unlikely to have the perspective to know (a) how important your work is, and (b) which journal is right for it, both in terms of subject matter and renown. You don't want to submit everything you write to the *Journal Where People Would Sell Their Souls to Be Published* (JWPWSTSTBP). You want to demonstrate to the editors of that journal that you are a good judge of your own work, that you're going to send them only your best stuff, and that you hope they'll consider it seriously when you do. On the other hand, you don't consistently want to aim too low and send all your work to the *Journal Known to Publish Grocery Lists* (JKTPGL), even if they were kind enough to publish your last paper after it had been rejected by three other journals.

Sometimes a journal's reputation for speed of publication (or lack thereof) will enter into the decision, particularly when a young researcher is feeling pressured to give his or her curriculum vitae some heft prior to a grant submission or job interview. Don't let the time factor inordinately influence you. You're almost always better off publishing in the best journal that will accept your work, even if it takes a bit longer. It is true, though, that if your paper is rejected by your first-choice journal, you'll need to re-tool the manuscript and resubmit it elsewhere, and this will take time. On average, the time from submission to publication will be about a year. Each submission, rejection, and resubmission cycle will add 6 to 12 months. So, that is a good reason to be realistic from the outset, and to aim somewhere with a decent chance of success.

Taking all of this information into consideration, how do you use it to make the important decision of where to submit your paper? This is where you turn to your research mentor for guidance. He or she will help you judge the merits of your work and pick a target journal whose readership will share your interest in the topic. Your choice should reflect a considered balance of likelihood of success with your willingness to tolerate failure— remembering that failure in scientific publishing is rarely absolute.

Gather Your Background Material. Perform a literature search to be sure that you are up to date with the most recent findings pertinent to your research. Don't rely on the information you gathered when you wrote your research proposal; chances are it's months (or, in some cases, years) out of date. It is especially important to repeat your literature search each time you revise and resubmit a paper. As noted above, this cycle can take many months (or longer), and new publications may have ensued in the interim. When you submit a manuscript to a journal, you want to ensure that your understanding of the topic, and your citation of references, is current. There is no better way to flag a recycled paper to journal referees (i.e., peer reviewers) or editors than to submit it with references that are patently ancient. This is a sign of carelessness that will give editors pause to wonder (and rightfully so!) if you were as lackadaisical in your conduct of the research as you were in writing it up. (This sounds harsh but, believe us, it's true.)

Decide on the Message. Before you set pen to paper (or fingers to key-board), you should ask yourself, "What is the message of this manuscript?" Having done all this work, completed the analyses, and thought a lot about the findings, what have you learned? More precisely, what do you want the reader to share of your experience? The message should be simple—this doesn't mean that persons uninitiated in the field will understand it, although persons knowledgeable in the area certainly should. Rather, identifying a simple message is a technique to help you distill what sometimes amounts to months (or, in some cases, years) of work into a few pages of text. No matter how detailed the methods, no matter how complicated the statistical analyses, as you write your paper you must constantly ask yourself, "What is the message?" and make this the paper's organizing principle.

Tell a Story. All good writing—fiction, nonfiction, and the special form of nonfiction that is the domain of science writing—tells a story. You must decide what story your research tells and then write it down. Your paper isn't a tale of how hard you worked, how smart you are, or how pleased you are with your accomplishments. It's the story of

- WHY you performed the research
- HOW you did it
- WHAT you found
- WHAT you think it means

This is a story that should be written succinctly, with candor, and with humility.

Why must you write succinctly? Journal space is precious, so scientific writing has to be lean. This doesn't mean it needs to be dull, it just means that it needs to be economical. Never say in 20 words what you can say in 10. Don't repeat in the Discussion section what you already covered in the Introduction. You will struggle to make everything fit into the allotted space. Journal editors love to say, "Please make the changes and additions recommended by the referees and, while you're at it, cut the size of your paper by 25%. Then we'll reconsider it for publication." Do yourself a favor and learn to write economically from the outset. (This takes practice and repeated to-and-fro of revisions with your mentor.)

Why must you write with candor? This, we hope, is obvious. The manuscript is the means by which you tell the world about your research endeavor. It needs to be scrupulously honest. You need to tell readers not only what you did, but what you did not do, and why. For example, it's not enough to say that you included 20 participants with schizophrenia in your study. Was it necessary for you to screen 120 persons with schizophrenia before you settled on the 20 who participated in your study? You must also say who was *not* included, and why. This is only one example of where candor is sacrosanct. Conscience must be your guide as to what you disclose to the reader. If you find yourself leaving out something *for a purpose,* take a deep breath and put that information in the manuscript.

Why must you write with humility? When you do research, you inevitably stand on the shoulders of giants. Give them due credit. Don't carp on the limitations of previous work without realizing that hindsight is 20/20. If your work is an advance, it is because others preceded you. And, you can be certain that others will follow you (soon!) and take your discovery a step further. So be humble, acknowledge forthrightly the limitations of your work, and recognize the contributions of earlier investigators—some of whom will undoubtedly be reviewing your manuscript!

Proofread. It is important, if not essential, that your manuscript be precise in its preparation. Perhaps worse than outdated reference to background materials is a manuscript that is full of careless errors. This is, indeed, a tell-tale sign that you may have been less than meticulous in other aspects of your research. The reviewers may wonder if a similar level of care was taken in collecting, cleaning, and analyzing data. This wonder may, or may not, be an accurate reflection of your overall level of care; if based on an error-filled manuscript, it is nothing less than warranted. So, be meticulous in formatting, in crafting sentences, in use of punctuation, in accuracy of all statements and statistical notations, in preparing references, and so on. Then proofread, make corrections, and proofread again. Realistically, even then a few typos and formatting errors may slide through but, of greatest importance, it will be obvious that you were vigilant.

Elements of a Peer-Reviewed Manuscript

Journals differ in the elements they require for publication. Check the "Instructions for Authors" for your target journal before you begin writing. Most journals in the social and medical sciences follow a similar format, consisting of the following components:

Title Page. This usually includes the title of the paper, the names and affiliations of the authors (though some journals ask you to provide a copy without this information to permit "blind" review of the paper, i.e., review of the paper without the referees knowing who the authors are), address and contact information for a corresponding author, and date of submission. Also included, either on this page or on supplementary pages, is information about source(s) of funding, acknowledgments, and disclosure of possible conflicts.

Abstract. This is usually of specified, finite length (typically 150–250 words), often formatted to include the required headings: Rationale (or Background), Methods, Results, and Conclusions. These correspond to the WHY (did we do the study), HOW (did we do the study), WHAT (did we find), and WHAT (does it mean) questions we outlined earlier in this chapter. Although some people like to write their Abstract when the rest of the paper is finished, we highly recommend writing the Abstract *first*. This approach forces you to decide very early in the writing process what the message of your paper will be and which critical pieces of information you will convey. Whenever we find ourselves getting lost or losing focus as we write a manuscript, we turn back to the Abstract to find our way.

Introduction. This is the part of the manuscript that puts your work in context. It should tell the reader why the topic is of importance or interest, what is and what is not known about it, and what you intended to do. Unlike a dissertation or grant proposal, or even a review article or chapter, it is not intended to be a comprehensive treatise on the subject. There simply is not enough room in a peer-reviewed article to accomplish this level of detail. Your goal, therefore, is to comment on the most important prior studies in this area, cite them, and set the stage for your study as the *next logical step* in the progression of this area of research.

Methods. This is the part of the paper where you describe the nuts and bolts of your research. Ideally, the level of detail should be such that a researcher outside of your lab would be able to read your Methods section and faithfully replicate your experiment(s). In reality, though, journal space limitations often preclude the provision of this level of detail. You can save space by referring to (and citing) methods that are standard in the field, leaving room for more detailed descriptions of methods that are unique to your work. Statistical methods should be outlined here, too. For studies that involve human participants, this is also the section of the paper where you describe the source and characteristics of study participants, and the fact that a suitable informed consent process was followed and documented.

Results. This is where you tell the reader what you found. Some authors prefer to begin this section with a description of the characteristics (e.g., age, gender, socioeconomic status) of their participants; others prefer to put this description in the Methods section. Next follows the actual presentation of the results of the study. These should be organized to correspond to the hypotheses you are testing. Most journals want you to present the data in sufficient detail that someone external to the process could check your analyses, if they so desired. As such, you should present not only measures of central tendency (e.g., means) but also measures of variability (e.g., standard deviation, or 95% confidence interval). Don't report "naked" p values (i.e., a p value that stands alone without mention of the statistical test value or degrees of freedom). Most journals require that you provide all of this information. For example, you might say, "Participants who preferred crunchy peanut butter ($N = 32$) watched more hours of professional wrestling per week on TV than did those who preferred smooth ($N = 41$; Mean hours watched = 12.7 [SD 3.4] vs. 0.3 [SD 0.2], $t = 20.6$, $df = 71$, $p < 0.0001$)." You should refrain from interpreting the data here; interpretation belongs in the Conclusions/Discussion section.

Conclusions (Sometimes Called Discussion or Comments). This is the part of the paper where you summarize your findings and attempt to help the reader interpret them. This is not a place to rehash the literature you may have cited in the Introduction; it is a place to comment on how your findings confirm, contradict, or expand upon those earlier studies. It is also a place to revisit your initial hypotheses and comment on the extent to which they have been disconfirmed by your findings. It is not a place to speculate wildly, but it may be a place to tentatively pose some new hypotheses. And, it is most definitely the place to itemize some of the limitations of your work, to comment on how these weaknesses might constrain interpretations of your work, and to propose how these shortcomings can be rectified in future studies.

Cover Letter. Although not, strictly speaking, part of the manuscript itself, the *cover letter* (i.e., the letter to the editor that accompanies your paper) is integral to the submission process. It should include the requisite information about the title of your paper, whom to contact about it, and so forth. Although a simple request that the manuscript be considered for publication is usually sufficient, we often prefer to provide the editor with a bit of information regarding the purpose of our study and why we feel the findings will be of interest to their readers. Some journals ask that you provide them with names of possible referees; these should be people who are expert in the area but are not your next of kin or people who owe you money. (Neither should they be people who hate your guts. It is legitimate to ask a priori that the paper not be submitted to a particular individual.) Many journals ask that all the authors sign the cover letter, though most accept that it is often logistically more convenient to have the corresponding author sign the letter and follow up as soon as possible thereafter with signed authorizations from all other authors.

Interpreting, Acting On, and Responding to an "Action" Letter

Some time (expect to wait a number of months) after submitting your manuscript, you will receive an *action letter* from the editor or one of the associate editors. This is a letter telling you what to do with your manuscript. Every journal uses a slightly different format for the letter, but they are generally trying to tell you one of four things:

Go Away and Don't Come Back. "We regret that we are unable to accept your paper for publication. It isn't (necessarily) a reflection of the quality of your work. Thank you for giving us the opportunity to review your paper. Good luck publishing it elsewhere."

This is a *rejection* letter. You are not being provided with an opportunity to fix the paper and resubmit it. In our experience, when you get this letter from an editor, it is best to move on and prepare your paper for submission to another journal. We have heard of authors who write back to the editor to say, "I think you are mistaken to have rejected my paper ...," but the returns from such an approach are bound to be vanishingly small. Editors think carefully before they reject a paper outright, and it seems unwise to question their judgment at such a fundamental level.

What should you do when you get a rejection letter? This is easy for us to say—and we admit that we rarely follow our own advice—but you should *not* take it personally. Early in your career, it is wise to talk with a mentor or supervisor who can help put it in perspective. In the vernacular of research as business, getting a paper rejected from a journal simply means that you didn't make the sale. This does not reflect on your intelligence or on your promise as a researcher. But, it can be particularly hard to handle when you get rejections early on. *Don't give up.* Read the critiques of the referees and do your best to correct whatever deficiencies you can. Then pick the "next best" target journal and submit it there. Rest assured that your paper will almost certainly (eventually) be published somewhere. You'll, no doubt, experience the "rush" of seeing your name and paper in print that keeps us coming back for more.

If You're Very Lucky, We May Eventually Publish Your Paper. "We would be willing to see a revised version of your paper. If you choose to resubmit, you must attend to the (one million and three) suggestions made by the referees. Undertaking such a revision will require considerable effort on your part, and acceptance cannot be guaranteed."

This is a *major revise and resubmit* letter. It means that the reviewers had some major questions or concerns about your paper, but not enough for the editor to kill it entirely. Whether or not it is accepted in its next iteration truly does depend on how successful you are at addressing the reviewers' comments and suggestions in a revised manuscript. In most cases, your resubmitted manuscript will undergo the scrutiny of one or more of the original peer reviewers in addition to that of the editor.

In our opinion, it is almost always worthwhile to make an earnest attempt at revising the manuscript, and resubmitting it. But, if you're going to do so, it is imperative that you go through the reviewer's comments—these will be provided for you along with the action letter—on a point-by-point basis and figure out (a) what you agree with and what you don't, and (b) what you can fix and what you can't. At times, serious and time-consuming re-analysis of the data is necessary. At other times, what is required is more of a re-interpretation of the findings combined with a willingness to acknowledge and cite alternative explanations for the results. In either case, you should be prepared to expend considerable effort on revising your manuscript.

When you resubmit your paper, you should include a cover letter that details, point by point, the changes you have made in the manuscript in response to specific referee critiques or suggestions. For example, you might say, "Reviewer #3 questioned our use of parametric statistics for the comparisons made in Table 2. We consulted with our biostatistician, who agreed that a nonparametric approach was preferable. We have revised Table 2 (p. 15 of the revised manuscript) accordingly." Providing this degree of detail makes the editor's job easier (a good idea, indeed!).

It is not essential that you agree with every point raised, nor is it critical that you make every change suggested. But if you *don't* do something that was recommended, you should be prepared to defend your choice in the cover letter. For example, you might say, "Reviewer #2 recommended that we re-analyze our data, excluding participants with blue eyes. Although we understand his or her rationale for this suggestion, we don't believe that this post hoc censoring of the data is warranted and have chosen not to follow this suggestion." But don't be argumentative. Don't say, "Reviewer #2 obviously ate a bad jalapeno before reviewing our paper. Consequently, we are choosing to ignore everything he or she said." Thank the reviewers and the editor for their suggestions.

We'll (Probably) Accept This Paper if You Fine-Tune It a Bit. Occasionally, the editor will tell you outright, "If you provide us with a revised manuscript that addresses the referees' comments, we will accept it for publication." But, more often than not, you'll get, "We would be delighted to see a revised version of your manuscript that addresses the comments made by the referees." For most journals, either of these messages means that your revised manuscript will not undergo re-review by outside referees. Rather, the editor or an associate editor will read it over to ensure that you've done what was asked and that the paper is now acceptable for publication. Acceptance is not guaranteed, but if you do your job and conscientiously revise the paper along the lines requested, your chances of acceptance are excellent (we think 80%–90%).

To revert once more to the "research as business" vernacular, a letter like this is money in the bank. Don't waste any time. Make the requested changes and resubmit (with a detailed cover letter, as described earlier in the section above) as quickly as possible.

Your Paper Is Accepted. "We are pleased to accept your paper for publication." Hallelujah! You've done it. It is rare, indeed, to get an unconditional letter of acceptance on the first try. No matter when it happens, it's sweet. Savor this one. Maybe even bronze it. You may not see its ilk for some time to come.

Summary

Writing a manuscript for peer review, and publishing it, can be a daunting experience for a novice researcher. But don't let your fear of failure stop you from trying. Turn to mentors and more senior colleagues for advice about where to publish, how to handle rejections, and where to resubmit. Dissemination of your findings through a professional, peer-reviewed journal marks the final step in your journey from question to hypothesis to experiment to results. Until you take that final step, your work is incomplete. When you write, keep a clear message in focus at all times. This will help you distill the many ingredients of your research experience into a concise, compelling story. Read your manuscript with a critical eye (applying some of the same strategies outlined in Chapter 4 for reading the work of others) and be wary of and correct errors in presentation. Tell this story with honesty and with the humility that comes from knowing that yours is just the latest version of a tale that has been and will be continuously rewritten.

Index

About the Authors

Gordon J. G. Asmundson, Ph.D., is currently Director of Clinical Research and Development at the Regina Health District, Saskatchewan, Canada. He is also an Adjunct Professor in the Department of Psychiatry, University of Saskatchewan, and the Departments of Psychology and Kinesiology and Health Studies, University of Regina. Dr. Asmundson has published more than 90 journal articles and book chapters, as well as an edited book. His research interests are in the areas of health service utilization, chronic pain, fear, and the anxiety disorders. He is married to Kimberley Asmundson, with whom he shares the love of their precious daughter, Aleiia.

G. Ron Norton, Ph.D., is currently Professor Emeritus at the University of Winnipeg, Manitoba, Canada. He also holds positions in the Departments of Psychology, PsycHealth, and Community Health Sciences at the University of Manitoba, Manitoba, Canada. Dr. Norton has published more than 100 scientific articles, primarily in the areas of anxiety disorders, substance abuse, and chronic pain. He has also published two previous books, *Parenting* (1976) and *Panic Disorder and Agoraphobia* (1991). He is married to Judith Norton and has two sons, Marshall and Peter. His younger son is following in his footsteps and will soon receive his Ph.D. in Clinical Psychology.

Murray B. Stein, M.D., F.R.C.P.C. is Professor of Psychiatry at the University of California San Diego and Director of the Anxiety & Traumatic Stress Disorders Programs at the Veterans Affairs San Diego Healthcare System. He is also an Adjunct Professor in the Department of Psychology at San Diego State University, and the Department of Psychiatry at the University of Manitoba. Dr. Stein has published more than 150 scientific articles and book chapters on the topic of anxiety disorders. He has also edited a book for professionals on Social Phobia, and has recently co-written a self-help book on this subject. His wife, Orah Stein, is also a physician, and they have three fabulous children, Rebecca, Nathan, and Dorit.

DATE DUE